FORD
Medium-Duty Trucks

1917-1998 Photo History

Paul G. McLaughlin

Enthusiast Books

www.enthusiastbooks.com

Library of Congress Control Number: 2005936379

ISBN-13: 978-1-58388-162-0
ISBN-10: 1-58388-162-X

Reprinted February 2018

Printed in USA

Copyediting by Suzie Helberg

Cover photo- 1948 Ford Cab-Over-Engine F-6 belonging to Myron Felix.

Table of Contents

Dedication

This book is dedicated to my wife Bernice who has supported me in all my projects and activities over the last 34 years. Her patience and understanding is truly appreciated; especially when I am working on one of these book projects, because everything else is put aside while I concentrate on doing my research and writing. Then there are all the trips I take to photograph trucks near and far away while she stays at home and takes my calls and saves all my messages. And I won't even go into how messy my office looks with stacks of reference materials piled high all over the place. She must love me because if she didn't she would have put her foot down a long time ago.

Paul G. McLaughlin

Acknowledgements

There are a number of people who assisted me in preparing and securing the material used in this book and I would like to take this opportunity to tell them how much I appreciated their help. They deserve some of the credit that moved this book project from an idea through to completion.

Bernice McLaughlin, Albuquerque, NM; Robert Lucero, DDS, Albuquerque, NM; Kenny Campbell, Albuquerque, NM; Eddie Corbin, Albuquerque, NM; Bill Fox, Johnson City, TN; Dennis Maag, St. Louis, MO; Dick Copello, York, PA; Larry Jones, Tijeras, NM; Dale Lewis, Stanley, NM; Fred Perkins, Weston, MA; John McLaughlin, Arlington, MA; Danny Melone, Weston, MA; George Hinds, Cambridge, MA; Jake Lewis, Stanley, NM; Archie Lewis, Moriarty, NM; Fred Sharf, Chestnut Hill, MA; Don Bunn, Bloomington, MN; Myron Felix, Cold Spring, MN; Archie Stutt, Hamilton, New Zealand; Guy Appelman, Albuquerque, NM; Jim Rowe, Twin Falls, ID; Larry Heister, Orting, WA; Charles Hess, Wadena, MN; Mike Gonzales, Albuquerque, NM; James Wagner, Detroit, MI; Shirley Sponholtz - *Old Time Trucks*; Michael MacSems, Olympia, WA; Vintage Truck Magazine, Yellow Springs, OH; J & R Auto Museum, Rio Rancho, NM; Tom Rostkowski, Placitas, NM; Jean Clarke, Woburn, MA; Lonney Kimmel, Albuquerque, NM; Amy Kimmel, Albuquerque, NM; Jessica McLaughlin, Albuquerque, NM; Paul C. McLaughlin, Rio Rancho, NM; P. J. McLaughlin, Rio Rancho, NM

Introduction

My interest in Ford trucks began at an early age back in the 1950s soon after my father began selling Ford cars and trucks. I remember going down to the dealership where he worked and playing in the back lot where the trucks were parked. And every now and then my father would take me on trips in those trucks to have bodies or equipment installed on them. Trips in those Ford trucks with my dad were special and made a lasting impression on me. Though a young boy at that time I promised myself that one day I would drive Ford trucks of my own. I have and I shall continue to do so.

As a Ford truck enthusiast I hope you will enjoy this book. Looking at these pictures brings back fond memories of Ford trucks I have seen and appreciated over the years. Some remind me of the trucks that I rode in with my dad so many years ago. Is it any wonder that I consider Ford trucks to be so special and enjoy writing about them?

Paul G. McLaughlin
Albuquerque, NM
January 2005

This Model TT Ford Chassis has been outfitted with an aftermarket sourced closed cab and body combination.

Chapter 1: Model TT Era 1917-1927

We all know that Henry Ford put America on wheels with his Model T Ford automobile. The reason why these cars were so popular is that they were rugged, dependable, easy to work on, economical, and they were relatively cheap to buy. With all those positive points is it any wonder that these cars shot to the top of the sales charts without too much trouble?

About the same time that Henry Ford was introducing his Model T to the automotive marketplace the fledgling trucking industry was starting to grow. With each and every passing year more horse-drawn wagons were being put out to pasture because motor trucks were replacing them. And supplying those trucks to this growing market were a number of different manufacturers offering trucks powered by gasoline or steam powered engines, or electric motors. Most of these trucks were on the pricey side with base prices ranging from $1,500 to $5,000, prices that might have deterred some buyers from getting a truck at that time.

During those early years Henry Ford concentrated his efforts on improving his cars but that didn't stop some of his cars from being used in the commercial truck business. In order to accomplish that feat a lot of Model T Ford owners who wanted a rugged, dependable, and low cost alternative to the high cost of trucking could modify their Model T cars into trucks by purchasing and installing a conversion kit that was designed to do just that. These kits were offered by a number of companies. The most famous of them were the Smith Form-A-Truck Company, Union Truck Manufacturing, Columbia, and the aptly named Truckford by the Eastern Truckford Company.

These kits usually included a pair of channel steel frame extenders, a semi-elliptic rear spring set, solid rubber rear tires mounted on heavy-duty steel artillery equipment wheels, a pair of chain sprockets to be mounted to the stock rear axle, a pair of chains, and a heavy-duty chain drive type rear axle.

The kits to modify Model T Ford cars into trucks started appearing on the market around 1911 or 1912 and the cost for one was around $350 to $400. At that price it made economic sense to convert a Model T Ford car into a truck rather than going out and buying a new truck from another manufacturer.

The truck business was growing by leaps and bounds during the 'teens and by the middle of the decade Henry Ford decided that he wanted a piece of this pie. After all, if the aftermarket could provide kits to convert his cars into trucks without too much cost or trouble, why couldn't he do the same thing? But instead of converting a car chassis to do the work of a truck he would design a new, real, truck chassis that could handle the rigors associated with a truck.

Henry Ford officially entered the truck business in July of 1917 when his company introduced the Model T Ton Truck Chassis, also known as the Model TT. This one-ton truck chassis emulated the various equipment that companies offered for converting Model T cars into trucks at that time. It differed from the Model T Car Chassis because of its longer and stronger frame rails, 2-foot longer

Here we see a Closed Cab Model TT Ford truck that has been equipped with a hand cranked towing setup.

This Model TT Ford truck in good condition is used by an antique store in Colorado to help promote its wares.

Another Model TT Truck with an Open Cab and Stake Body. Note that this truck features a matched set of wooden spoke wheels front and back.

wheelbase, stiffer rear springs, artillery type rear wheels, solid rubber rear truck tires, and a worm gear type of rear axle. The front tires on this chassis were of a 30 x 3-inch size in a pnuematic form while the rear tires were a 32 x 3-inch size in a solid rubber form.

With the introduction of this new Ford factory-built truck chassis demand for the aftermarket conversion kits declined; however, some people still bought them to convert older Model T cars into trucks. In order to stay in business some of those companies developed conversion kits that could turn a Model TT truck chassis into a chassis that could be rated at 1½ or even 2 tons.

The price for one of these Model T One-Ton Truck Chassis was $600 f.o.b. Detroit in the early years of production. For that amount of money, besides the one-ton rated chassis, you received the same 4-cylinder engine and planetary transmission used in Model T cars, a gas tank, short running boards, a dashboard, radiator, engine hood, front fenders, electric headlights, and an oil fired taillight. Like pricing on the Model T car, which dropped over the years, the price of the Model T

One-Ton Truck Chassis would drop from a high of $600 in 1917 to as low as $350 by the end of the Model T era in 1927.

Around 1920 or so people started referring to these Model T trucks as "Model TT" trucks, with that "TT" designation standing either for "Ton Truck" or "T Truck." In the same year demountable rear wheel rims and pneumatic rear tires were offered as extra cost options on the Model TT truck chassis. An electric starter and generator were offered as options on these Ford trucks starting in 1922, and in 1923 a high speed rear axle option was offered as a complement to the standard rear axle.

When Henry Ford entered the truck business in 1917 he wasn't the only one who was offering factory built trucks to the market. During the Model T era there were hundreds of companies around the country offering trucks but by the mid-1920s 3/4 of the trucks in use had a Ford TT Chassis underneath them. Some companies, like the Graham Brothers Company, used the Ford built chassis and running gear under their own trucks. The Graham Brothers Company used the basic Model T One-Ton Chassis under some of their trucks in the late 'teens before the company was bought out by the Dodge Brothers.

From the time he entered the truck business in 1917 until 1924 Henry Ford and his dealers sold the Model T One-Ton Truck Chassis without a cab or body. Henry felt that he didn't want to compete against all the aftermarket companies that were supplying cabs and bodies that were installed on his truck chassis. Besides, even though he didn't offer a complete truck to his buyers, he still sold a very high number of Model T One-Ton Truck Chassis. In 1923 alone his company produced 193,200 Model T One-Ton Truck Chassis here in the USA and Canadian production added another 32,000 units to that total.

That attitude changed in 1924 when Henry Ford decided the time was right to offer factory built Ford trucks with cabs and bodies already installed in addition to his separate Model T One-Ton Truck Chassis. So now a buyer could buy just the chassis at his Ford dealer or a cab with his chassis, or a complete truck, without having to go anywhere else.

Ford called the cab they used an "Open Cab" and it was done in a "C" cab style that was popular with truck manufacturers and buyers of that time. It was called a "C" cab because from the side the cab opening looked like the letter "C." These all-steel Ford cabs came with doors on both sides and a steel top that mounted to the cab and top of the windshield. It also came with a large, two-piece safety glass windshield in front and a small oval rear window on the back of the top. The upper sides of the cab were open and offered very little protection from the elements. However, one could order a set of canvas and mica snap-on side curtains, which offered some protection from snow and rain, and cold weather. These curtains were used mostly in the months with cold weather and removed during the rest of the year to provide air circulation into and around the cab.

Besides those new "C" cabs the Ford Motor Company started to offer their own factory bodies in 1924. The most popular factory-supplied body for these Model TT trucks was an all-steel body that Ford referred to as the "Express Body." This body was basically a long, shallow pickup truck type box and it came with a set of rear fenders at no extra cost. This complete truck was available for $490 f.o.b. Detroit. Compare that price to the price of a Model TT truck chassis, which in 1924 was priced around $370. If you wanted a cover for that "Express Body" Ford could supply that too. Ford called this cover a canopy and charged $30 for it. If you wanted side curtains and screens they were available at a cost of $40 including the canopy. When all those costs were added up you had a pretty neat little truck. These Canopied Express Ford Trucks were pretty popular with street peddlers who liked to carry

This 1917 Model T Ton Truck features an aftermarket body that resembles the early "jitney" bus bodies that were popular in the early part of the twentieth century.

fruits and vegetables, which they could distribute to customers along their routes. They were also popular with municipalities who liked to use them as dogcatcher vehicles.

The following year of 1925 would be an even better year for Ford truck buyers because of some new factory product offerings from the company. The biggest news about a new product revolved around a new steel closed cab model. This "Closed Cab" model included glass windows in the doors that were raised or lowered through the use of some woven cloth straps, a windshield that could be opened for ventilation in the warm weather, a rubber floor mat, and a dispatch (glove) box in the dashboard. Equipped like this these Closed Cab Fords cost the buyer $85, which was $20 more than what Ford charged for a Model TT Open Cab. The Closed Cab Model TT trucks also featured removable rear cab panels that could be taken out to facilitate access from inside the cab into the body area and vice versa if need be.

Popcorn wagons like this unit on a Model TT chassis were popular sights on city streets in the USA back 75 or 80 years ago.

Besides their new Closed Cab Model TT truck Ford also introduced a new light-duty truck model (Ford called it a Commercial Car), which would set the stage for millions to follow. This new model was the grandfather of America's number 1 selling vehicle for the last 28 years, the F Series Ford Pickup. This new model made its official debut on April 25, 1925. Ford called it a Model T Runabout with Pickup Body. In the Ford sales catalog that year it was listed as costing $281 f.o.b. Detroit. For that price the Ford truck buyer got a sporty looking pickup truck that used a steel box that was quite a bit shorter than the pickup truck box that was used on the Model TT Express. Though this new Ford truck was only on the market a short period of time Ford still managed to sell almost 34,000 of them before the sales year was done.

The shorter pickup box on this Runabout Ford was perfect for small businesses and for hauling small loads while the longer Express Body was designed to carry larger, longer, and heavier loads. As we said earlier Henry Ford considered the Runabout with Pickup Body a Commercial Car rather than a regular truck like the Model TT Express, and with both types of vehicles in his lineup he had the light-duty and medium-duty markets covered.

Henry Ford prided himself on being able to offer low cost vehicles to the market. In the chart below you can see the prices he charged for his products in 1925. All listed prices are f.o.b. Detroit, which meant that you might have to pay extra for shipment of the vehicle to your destination.

Model TT Truck Prices as of July 1925

One-Ton Truck Chassis	$365
Closed Cab with Express Body	$505
Closed Cab with Express Body and Canopy	$535
Closed Cab with Express Body, Canopy, and Side Screens	$560
Open Cab with Express Body	$430
Open Cab with Express Body and Canopy	$515
Open Cab with Express Body, Canopy, and Side Screens	$540

In February of 1925 Ford added another truck body to his catalog of Model TT Trucks. This factory-built body was called a Platform Body in an 8 x 5-foot size. The body itself consisted of a series of Southern Pine boards that were joined together to provide a strong floor to carry heavy loads. These boards were then placed into a steel frame that included holes for stake panels. When this body was ordered with stakes it was referred to in the catalog as a Stake Body. When ordered with an open cab a Stake Bodied Model TT Ford truck retailed for $495 while a similar Stake Body ordered with a Closed Cab cost $515.

Since he had grown up on a farm Henry Ford felt that the Platform and Stake Body Ford Model TT trucks would be perfect for farmers and he heavily promoted them to farmers through magazines and newspapers that catered to farming, including magazines like *Successful Farmer* and the *Country Gentleman*. Whenever you saw photographs of these trucks being used on farms they were usually overloaded, especially when they were hauling hay. In most of the magazine and newspaper ads that featured Model TT Fords in a farm setting Ford also promoted his Fordson tractor. A Model TT Ford truck and a Fordson tractor made for an unbeatable combination back in those early days of mechanized farming.

Though his Model TT trucks were selling well Henry Ford gave some thought to producing some heavier-duty trucks as well—trucks that could handle 2- and 3-ton loads. As far as we know the 3-ton truck concept never got off the drawing board but a 2-ton Ford truck actually made it to the prototype stage. Though it was not called a Model TT Ford truck it used mostly Model TT parts in its construction. Now this 2-ton rated Ford truck was called a Fordson and some of them were actually built for testing purposes. As far as we can tell one of these trucks was actually sold to a friend of Henry Ford and it is still in existence to this day.

Before we leave this chapter we have to say a few words about other popular Ford based trucks of this period. Those were the Ford Model T and Model TT Fire Trucks that were seen in just about every single city, town, and hamlet during the Model T era. Fire fighting equipment manufacturers loved the Ford Model T and Model TT Chassis because they were cheap to buy, rugged, and dependable. They also liked them because of their high ground clearance, which enabled them to go anywhere to fight a fire. Most of them were small and agile so they could get into tight places that larger fire engines couldn't, which made them popular with fire fighters. Untold numbers of these chassis were bought and converted to fire fighting duty and many of them can still be seen today in parades and fire station displays.

This Model TT Open Cab truck is wearing an aftermarket type wooden express body.

Now here is a different use of a Model T Ford truck chassis. It is equipped with a circus style Calliope body. Note the circus paintings on its side.

School bus bodies were mounted on a number of Model AA Chassis like the 1929 model shown here.

Chapter 2: An Improved Model AA Steps In to Replace the Model TT 1928-1931

At the beginning of the 1920s decade Henry Ford was in the driver's seat as far as automobile manufacturers were concerned. His Model T Ford was the most popular car in the world and his Model TT trucks were fast approaching the same mark if they were not there already. At this point the Ford Motor Company and Henry Ford were at the top of their game but by the middle of the decade Henry and his company were starting to lose their grip and the competition was making deep cuts into their sales leadership.

Automobile buyers were becoming more sophisticated and demanding more comforts and conveniences in their cars. While the competition was constantly making improvements to their products Henry Ford decided to stay with the status quo. Those improvements increased the costs of his competition's products while the costs of Henry Ford's vehicles actually decreased over the years. Henry thought, rightly or wrongly, that low prices were more important to buyers than the latest gimmicks. Henry had the competition beat on prices but he was falling behind in matters of safety, styling, and other categories that were becoming more important to buyers.

Henry tried to improve the Model T and Model TT Fords by refining their styling and adding more accessories. But in the end he finally agreed with his critics that the days of the Model T era were coming to an end. In May or June of 1927 he pulled the plug on his beloved Model T and Model TT by shutting down production and closing his plants so that they could get ready to begin producing a worthy successor to the Model T Ford.

In his heart Henry Ford knew that this new Ford had to be better than the Model T it replaced if he was ever to recapture that Ford magic that had served him so well for almost 20 years. This new Ford, both car and truck, would have to be more stylish, safer to operate, more powerful, better equipped, and be easier to use than its predecessor.

Ford called this new vehicle a Model A, a revived name that had served Ford well when it was applied to early cars built by the Ford Motor Company in 1903. It went into production in early November 1927 and a month or so later millions of Americans got to see this new Ford when it made its debut in thousands of Ford showrooms across the nation in early December.

This new Ford shared very little with the Model T it replaced. It was more stylish, sportier, and a lot easier to drive than Ford's earlier cars. On the truck side of the ledger the new Ford trucks were called Model AAs and they too were much improved over what was offered previously from Ford.

Once again these trucks were offered in Open or Closed Cab models. The Open Cab trucks utilized a new, more stylish body while the Closed Cab trucks used a carryover modified TT style of cab. These all-steel cabs were fitted out just like the earlier Model TT versions except now the windows in the doors used roll up mechanisms rather than cloth straps to perform the open and closed

Here is a promotional vintage photograph showing a specialized cab and body that has been mounted on a Model AA Chassis.

functions. The Open Cab version still used a canvas top like the Model TT snap-on side curtains that were available to help keep the elements from getting into the cab.

Both types of trucks used the same front fenders, cowl panel, hood, radiator shell, and headlight buckets that were used on the Model A Ford cars. The only difference between the Model A and the Model AA, like the headlight buckets and the radiator shell, was that they were painted in black enamel rather than being finished in a stainless steel, as on the cars. Some owners of these trucks did dress them up a bit by buying the brightly finished car parts and transferring them to their trucks.

All Model A and Model AA vehicles now used a gravity feed gas tank that was mounted up underneath the cowl panel rather than under a seat, which made the refueling job, thanks to an external mounted cap, much easier. Also all Model A and Model AA vehicles now had four-wheel brake systems that made them a lot safer to operate.

The Model AA Ford truck, as the Model TT before it, used a bigger and more powerful 4-cylinder engine. It displaced 200 cubic inches and carried a horsepower rating of 40 horsepower at 2,200 rpm. The power output was almost double what the Model TT offered. Besides being more

Check out the long overhang on the back of this bus which appears to be installed on a 1931 Ford Model AA Chassis.

powerful this engine featured a much improved oiling system and an improved cooling system as well. Both the new Model A and Model AA vehicles used a new 3 forward speed "H" shift pattern manual transmission that was controlled by a floor mounted lever rather than the pedal operated planetary style transmission used on earlier Fords. As an added bonus a 1928 Ford Model AA truck buyer could order an auxiliary transmission from the factory that effectively doubled the

Here is a nifty example of a 1930 Model AA Ford with a hand cranked dump body.

gear choices. Ford called this optional extra-cost transmission a "Dual High" transmission. It was basically a 2-speed planetary transmission that was mounted behind the regular transmission. Two pedals mounted in the cab controlled it and when in use the driver had a choice of six forward and two reverse speeds.

The Model AA truck chassis was designed and engineered to be a lot stronger than the Model TT chassis it replaced. So much so that these new trucks were now rated at 1½ tons rather than 1 ton. These Model AA chassis used frame rails that were larger and thicker than earlier versions. They also incorporated a heavier-duty front transverse mounted spring with shock absorbers and heavier-duty rated longitudinal cantilever type leaf springs on the back. The Model AA trucks used car type front brake drums and special truck style 14-inch drums on the rear. All 1928 Ford Model AA trucks used 20-inch welded spoke wheels. Those wheels were fitted with 30 x 5-inch tires on the front and 32 x 6-inch tires on the back. Both sets of wheels used high-pressure truck tires that were retained on the wheel by locking rings.

These Model AA trucks now featured a 131½-inch wheelbase, a two-piece driveshaft, and the choice of either a heavy-duty bevel gear type rear end or a heavy-duty version of a worm gear type rear end. Gear ratios offered were either a low 7.16:1 or a higher geared 5.11:1.

Standard color paint on the 1928 cab, cowl, and hood was a dark green lacquer, which was combined with a black enamel that was applied on the wheels, fenders, radiator shells, running boards, and headlight buckets.

When the Model AA trucks made their debut in early 1928 you could buy just a Model AA chassis for around $460. The following chart shows the different models and their codes that were offered in the Model AA line of 1928.

1928 Model AA Trucks And Codes

Open Cab	Type 76-A
Closed Cab	Type 82-A
Express Body	Type 89-A
Platform Body	Type 88-A
Stake Body	Type 188-A

Later on in the model year Ford decided to go after the covered cargo market by offering two new Panel Delivery models. One, the Type 79-A, was the smaller version that was based on the Commercial Car Model A Chassis. The other version, the larger model Type 85-A, was based on the 131½-inch wheelbase Model AA Chassis. Budd Manufacturing supplied both types of bodies to Ford assembly plants across the USA. These bodies were shipped in knocked-down subassemblies that were assembled and painted on site by Ford employees. Both trucks featured steel bodies with rubberized fabric roofs that were mounted to wooden frames. These trucks came equipped with two bucket seats and dual vertical rear doors. Trucks like these were meant to appeal to grocers, cleaners, and other businesses that specialized in door-to-door home deliveries.

About the same time these new Panel Delivery models were making their debut the Ford Motor Company announced that they were going to offer new, factory built School Bus models in their catalog. The shorter version of these buses could accommodate about 9 passengers while the larger of the two could seat about 15 passengers. Both types featured wooden framed bodies that were covered in steel and the roofs were once again covered in a rubberized fabric material. They also used long bench type seats that could be folded up when not in use. Access was provided through a rear door along with regular access through the right front door. If a customer didn't want to purchase a Ford built school bus he could always purchase a Model AA Truck Chassis and have his own choice of bodies installed.

In this period photograph we see a passenger bus body that has been mounted on a 1930 or 1931 Model AA Chassis.

When all was said and done the 1928 Ford Model AA trucks were better vehicles than what was offered before in the Model TT versions. Though these were good trucks in their own right Henry Ford was not ready to start resting on his laurels. For the 1929 model year he set out to make the good even better. The first improvement came about soon after the 1929 models were introduced when Ford changed the wheel design on the Model AA trucks from a welded spoke design to a heavier-duty steel wheel with a 6-hole disc design.

Later on in the model year, around October, Ford made a few more changes to make its Model AA trucks even better. The first big change involved the transmission, which was changed from a 3-speed to a 4-speed unit. When Ford instituted this change they did away with the "Dual-High" transmission option.

Around the same time that the transmission change was taking place Ford changed the Model AA's worm drive type rear axle to a heavier-duty rated spiral bevel design. Along with this change Ford also fitted these trucks with beefed up front axles, radius rods, springs, king pins, and axle bear-

This 1931 Model AA Ford Closed Cab tow truck looks neat with all its period accessories.

ings. These new front axle setups were also treated to a set of larger front brake drums, thereby increasing the efficiency of the total braking system.

Ford's 6-hole steel disc wheels were changed again to a new 5-hole design. These wheels were now wrapped up in a set of 6-ply balloon tires in a new 6 x 20-inch size.

By the end of the 1929 model year Ford's truck sales set a new record of more than 355,400 units; a sales record that would stand for a number of years.

The 1930 model year for Ford Model AA trucks started later than the previous model years. These new Ford trucks didn't make their debut until June 1930, which was about six months later than normal. That late debut might have had something to do with a restyling job that mimicked the restyling job done on the Ford Model A cars. These new Fords featured a redesigned cowl panel that was a bit taller than the earlier versions. That higher cowl panel matched a new taller hood along with a taller, and narrower, radiator shell.

Once again these trucks were offered in Open Cab and Closed Cab models and the latter featured a new, more stylish, design.

For those customers who wanted a longer chassis for mounting longer bodies Ford added a new longer wheelbase chassis to their Model AA truck mix. Now buyers had a choice between a 131½-inch wheelbase truck and one with a longer 157-inch wheelbase. That longer wheelbase was used with a chassis whose overall length was 223 inches as compared to the shorter chassis that was about 183 inches long.

Another change seen on the Model AA truck chassis this year was an optional dual wheel design rear axle setup.

Besides all of these changes Henry Ford decided to increase his share of the 1930 truck market by offering even more factory cataloged models this year. All totaled Ford offered 28 different versions of his Model AA trucks. These models ranged from the Model AA Truck Chassis to a hydraulically powered dump truck with a Galion built body (Model Type 208-A). This was one of seven dump truck bodies that Ford offered that year. In addition to all these dump truck bodies Ford offered a number of coal bodies, garbage truck bodies, coal and dump truck combination bodies, and, of course, their regular Express, Platform, Stake, School Bus, and Panel Delivery trucks.

1930 Model AA Truck Models

Type	Description
76-A	Open Cab
76-B	Open Cab
82-A	Closed Cab
82-B	Closed Cab
85-B	Panel Delivery
88-A	Platform
89-A	Express
185-A	Platform 157-inch Wheelbase
186-A	Stake 157-inch Wheelbase
188-A	Stake 131½-inch Wheelbase
200-A	Hand Cranked Anthony Built Dump Body
201-A	Coal Body with Hydraulic Lift (75 cu. ft. cap.)
201-B	Coal Body with Hydraulic Lift with Sides By Wood (75 or 120 cu. ft. cap.)

201-C Coal Body with Hydraulic Lift by Wood Company (75 cu. ft. cap.)

202-A Anthony Gravity Feed Dump Body

203-A Galion Garbage Body with Hydraulic Lift (2 cu. yard cap.)

203-B Wood Built Garbage Body with Hydraulic Lift (2 cu. yard cap.)

203-C Galion Built Garbage Body with Hydraulic Lift (3 cu. yard cap.)

203-D Wood Built Garbage Body with Hydraulic Lift (3 cu. yard cap.)

204-A Galion Dump Body with Light-Duty Hydraulic Lift (1-1/2 cu. yard cap.)

205-A Hi-Lift Body by Wood Company with Hydraulic Lift (72 cu. ft. cap.)

206-A Anthony Built Rotary Power Hoist Dump Body

207-B Dump and Coal Body Combination with Hydraulic Lift (1-1/2 cu. yard or 120 cu. ft. cap. with wooden side boards attached)

208-A Galion Dump Body with Heavy-Duty Hydraulic Lift

208-B Wood Built Dump Body with Heavy-Duty Hydraulic Lift (1-1/2 cu. yard cap.)

236-A Light-Duty Hydraulic Lift with understructure equip. by Galion

237-A Light-Duty Hydraulic Lift with understructure equip. by Galion

330-A School Bus

This Ford Model AA Closed Cab truck with Stake Body has been dressed up with a car type stainless steel radiator shell.

A Ford Model AA Closed Cab truck with a Ford Service Truck Body is shown in this promotional vintage photograph.

Though Ford offered his truck customers more choices in factory supplied bodies Model AA truck sales were down this year. This downturn was probably the result of worsening economic conditions in the second year of the Great Depression, rather than a negative reaction by the public to these redesigned trucks. Even though sales were down Ford still retained its top position on the sales charts again this year.

Once again Ford's truck marketing strategy for the 1931 model year was to offer its truck buyers even more factory cataloged choices than what was offered the year before. Ford listed 50 different Model AA truck variations this year. Those variants ranged from a simple Model AA Truck Chassis to a fancy, low production Funeral Coach Body. A number of outside companies supplied these bodies to Ford assembly plants. Companies like Galion, Wood, Budd, Briggs, Murray, Midland Steel, Baker-Raulang, and others.

Besides the regular 131½ and 157-inch wheelbase models Ford added a new shorter wheelbase

Ford's Traveling Shows that crisscrossed this country were very popular affairs back in the 1930s. This photograph shows such a show back in 1931.

model to their truck mix. This one was a dropped-frame type chassis that featured a 112-inch wheelbase. This shorter length wheelbase and chassis was a perfect size for stand-up delivery vehicles similar to the type that milkmen and other door-to-door delivery companies used. Ford even offered one of its own specialized vehicles in this category. Ford called this special model a Standrive Delivery. Baker-Raulang supplied this body to Ford and the whole truck was priced at an appealing $1,050. At that price it was cheaper than other similar vehicles on the market at that time.

Ford wanted to expand their market share in the truck business even further this year and their truck group came up with some slick looking vehicles for even more specialized market niches. How specialized you might say? How about two funeral vehicles based on Ford's DeLuxe Panel Trucks; a plain and a fancy version. The plain wrapper model was a 3-door truck called a Funeral Service Car (Type 270-A) and it came equipped with a lot of standard items at no extra cost. It featured items like a flower tray, genuine leather covered seats, window covers, casket rollers, cowl lamps, bright plated front bumper, stainless steel headlamp buckets, cowl band trim, spoke type wire

wheels, and a bright plated radiator shell. Priced at $1,550 f.o.b. Detroit it was one of the priciest Model AA trucks produced that year, which might explain why Ford only produced 17 of them that year. As you can imagine they were extremely rare back then and are nearly impossible to find today.

Briggs was the company that supplied these fancy bodies to Ford and they also supplied a fancier version as well. Ford called this version a Funeral Coach (Type 275-A). This one came with more standard features and was priced right around $2,000. For that extra $450 dollar investment this truck came with such amenities as side window curtains, four doors, casket rollers and stops, an interior covered in rich mohair materials, wire spoke wheels, heavy-duty rear springs, stainless steel trim, a removable center pillar to facilitate side loading, and rear shock absorbers for a smoother ride. With a total production of between 75 and 95 units, this truck wasn't a big seller for Ford either.

For those who wanted to supply emergency treatment to patients or transportation of the same Ford offered another DeLuxe Panel variant called the Ambulance (Type 280-A). Like the Funeral Coach, DeLuxe Panel, and Funeral Service Car the Ambulance used a Briggs supplied Ford body. This 5-door model differed from the others in the specialized equipment it came with. Standard equipment on these Ambulances included a stretcher, spring loaded gurney, a bed with mattresses, attendant seats, chrome-plated interior trimmings, white lacquer painted interior and exterior, folding rear steps, a medicine cabinet, safety glass in all window areas, interior cooling fans, steel spoke wheels, and a buzzer to signal the driver. Ford produced about 80 of these Ambulances in 1931 and they were sold for $1,800 each. Since these vehicles and the Funeral models were not all that popular they were dropped after the 1931 model year.

Murray was another body supplier to Ford at this time and in 1931 they had a couple of specialized bodies that were created for law enforcement duties. Both vehicles were based on the Model AA 131½-inch wheelbase chassis. The first vehicle was called the Standard Police Patrol and some of its special features included a separation panel between the driver's compartment and the prisoner section, a rear step, a pull down rear security door, steel disc wheels, side windows, and wooden benches for the prisoners and guards to sit on. Suggested retail price for this model was $925 and Ford produced about 120 of them, which was about three times as many as they produced of the DeLuxe Police Patrol models. This was the other Murray supplied law enforcement model that Ford sold that year.

This version came with cowl lamps, a stainless steel cowl trim band, stainless steel headlight buckets, wire spoke wheels, stainless steel front bumper, a stainless steel radiator shell, first aid kit, rear area dome light, fancier trimmed driver's compartment, mounted gun rack, a signaling buzzer, and wooden benches for the prisoners and guards to sit on.

In August of 1931 Ford introduced a new, all steel, closed cab for Closed Cab models. Prior to the introduction of this new cab all Closed Cab Model A and Model AA trucks used a roof panel with a rubberized cloth covered material. But now that rubberized cloth panel was a thing of the past because of Ford's use of an all-steel roof panel.

When all was said and done Henry Ford accomplished what he set out to do. He produced a series of trucks and cars that were better than the vehicles they replaced. These Model A and Model AA vehicles were even more popular than the Model T and Model TT vehicles they replaced but their production run would be a lot shorter than the production run of the Model T. Instead of a 19-year production run the Model A and Model AA Fords would only carry the Ford banner for 4 years because the buying public at the time was demanding even more from the automobile manufacturers and Henry Ford could ill afford to fall

Model A Fords are popular with hot rodders but this hot rodder built himself something unique—a hot rodded Model AA School Bus.

This 1928-1929 Model AA Ford truck has a special custom body mounted to its frame.

You don't see too many of these around anymore. An Open Cab 1931 Model AA Ford truck with a Stake body.

Back in their day U.S. Mail Model AA trucks were probably a common sight on the streets. This is the only one your author has ever seen.

behind his competition in this very competitive market.

1931 Model AA Truck Models

Type	Description
76-B	Open Cab
82-B	Closed Cab
85-B	Panel Delivery (131½-inch Wheelbase)
185-B	Platform (157-inch Wheelbase)
186-B	Stake (157-inch Wheelbase)
187-A	Platform (131½-inch Wheelbase)
189-A	Stake (131½-inch Wheelbase)
195-A	Express (131½-inch Wheelbase)
196-A	Canopy Top and Screens with Express Body
197-A	Express Body (157-inch Wheelbase)
199-A	Ice Wagon
200-B	Galion Dump Body with Hand Crank (1½ yard cap.)
201-A	Galion Built Coal Body with Heavy-Duty Hydraulic Lift (75 cu. ft. cap.)
201-B	Wood Built Coal Body with Heavy-Duty Hydraulic Lift and Swinging Partition (75 cu. ft. or 120 cu. ft. cap.)
201-C	Wood Built Coal Body with Heavy-Duty Hydraulic Lift (75 cu. ft. cap.)
202-B	Wood Built Gravity Feed Dump Body
203-A	Galion Built Garbage Body with Heavy-Duty Hydraulic Lift
203-B	Wood Built Garbage Body with Hydraulic Lift
203-C	Galion Built Garbage Body with Hydraulic Lift (3 cu. yard cap.)
203-D	Wood Built Garbage Body with Hydraulic Lift (3 cu. yard cap.)
204-A	Galion Built Dump Body with Light-Duty Hydraulic Lift
204-B	Wood Built Dump Body with Light-Duty Hydraulic Lift
205-A	Wood Built High Lift Coal Body (72 cu. ft. cap.)

206-B Detwiller Built Dump Body with Hand Crank Lift
207-B Combination Dump and Coal Body with High Sides
208-A Galion Built Dump Body with Heavy-Duty Hydraulic Lift
208-B Wood Built Dump Body with Heavy-Duty Hydraulic Lift
210-A Panel Delivery
228-A Farm Body with Stock Racks
236-A Galion Built Body with Light-Duty Hydraulic Lift
236-B Body with Light-Duty Hydraulic Lift
237-A Heavy-Duty Hydraulic Lift Body with understructure by Galion
237-B Heavy-Duty Hydraulic Lift Body with understructure by Wood
238-A Farm Body with Stock Racks (157-inch Wheelbase)
239-A Meat Packers Express Body
242-A Heavy-Duty Express Body (131½-inch Wheelbase)
244-A Grain Body (157-inch Wheelbase)
248-A Grain Body (131½-inch Wheelbase)
330-A School Bus
330-B Passenger Bus
270-A Funeral Service Car
300-A DeLuxe Panel
290-A Standard Police Patrol
285-A DeLuxe Police Patrol
280-A Ambulance
275-A Funeral Coach
229-A Service Car or DeLuxe Express Body
AA-131 Chassis (131½-inch Wheelbase)
AA-112 Chassis (112-inch Wheelbase)
315-A Standrive Delivery Vehicle

The Railway Express Agency is long gone as are Ford Model AA Open Cab trucks like this 1931 example shown here.

This sharp looking 1931 Ford Model AA truck with Platform Body looks like it could still do a day's work without too much fuss.

This photograph shows a rear 3/4 view of a 1932 Ford dump truck that is undergoing restoration.

Chapter 3: A New Age, New Power, and New Models 1932-1939

Though the Model T Fords that preceded them were in production for 19 years Henry Ford's Model A and Model AA vehicles came to the end of their run in March of 1932. Just a little over four years had elapsed from when they were introduced. Even though these vehicles were much better than the Model T Henry Ford knew that he had to outdo himself if he was to remain competitive in this new marketplace of the 1930s. What was good before needed to be even better now.

People thought that Henry Ford had outdone himself when he introduced his new Model B and Model BB trucks in March 1932. Then a few weeks later he announced that he would be releasing a new V-8 engine in his cars. His 4-cylinder cars would still be called "Model B" Fords while the same car with a V-8 under the hood would be called a "Model 18." The number "1" indicated a first of a car and the "8" referred to its V-8 engine.

At first Henry Ford restricted the V-8 engine to his automobiles but by the end of the model year this option was extended to all Ford cars and trucks. The number of V-8 engines originally installed in 1932 Ford Model BB trucks is rather low. However, a number of these trucks were retrofitted with Ford V-8 engines in subsequent years through Ford's Rebuilt Engine Exchange Program.

Ford's Model BB trucks featured redesigned front-end parts like the hood, radiator shell, fenders, and a redesigned cab. These trucks came with larger gas tanks (17 gallons versus 11 gallons on the Model AA) and this tank was once again carried under the front seat.

These restyled trucks now sat on beefier frames with improved steering and braking systems. They also came equipped with a new torque-tube style rear axle that was independently sprung on a set of semi-elliptic springs. Model BB truck frames were still available in wheelbases of 131½ inches and 157 inches for those who needed to run a longer body.

The new Ford V-8 engine displaced 221 cubic inches and it carried a gross horsepower rating of 65 at 3,400 rpm. An improved 4-cylinder engine still displacing 200 cubic inches was now rated at 50 horsepower in 1932. The price of a V-8 engine in a 1932 Ford vehicle was $60.

1932 Ford BB Truck Lineup

Type	Description
BB-2	Closed Cab (157-inch Wheelbase)
BB-85	Standard and DeLuxe Panel Deliveries (131½-inch Wheelbase)
BB-210	Standard and DeLuxe Panel Deliveries (157-inch Wheelbase)
186-B	Stake Body (157-inch Wheelbase)
185-B	Platform Body
238-A	Platform Body with Stock Racks
244-A	Grain Tight Farm Body
187-A	Platform (131½-inch Wheelbase)
189-A	Stake Body (131½-inch Wheelbase)
248-A	Grain Body (131½-inch Wheelbase)
228-A	Stock Racks Body (131½-inch Wheelbase)
BB-195	Express Body (131½-inch Wheelbase)
BB-196	Express Body with Canopy (131½-inch Wheelbase)
BB-197	Large Standard Express Body (157-inch Wheelbase)
242-A	Closed Cab Heavy-Duty Express (131½-inch Wheelbase)

The Automobile Club of Southern California is printed on the sides of the doors of this 1932 Ford tow truck that is on display in the Petersen Automobile Museum in Los Angeles.

A 3/4 front view of a 1932 Ford dump truck. The V-8 emblem on the front of the grille indicates that this truck is powered by a 221-cubic-inch Flathead Ford V-8.

A later model 1935 or 1936 grille and radiator shell have been installed on this Ford truck cab which looks to be a 1933 or so model.

Trucks don't get much prettier than this 1934 Ford V-8 Closed Cab model with a Platform Body.

BB-208A	Galion All-Steel Dump Body with Hydraulic Lift and a Closed Cab
BB-204A	Closed Cab with a Wood Built Dump Body with Hydraulic Lift
BB-208B	Closed Cab with Galion Built Body with Hydraulic Lift
BB-204B	Closed Cab with Wood Built Dump Body
BB-200	Closed Cab Dump Truck Body with Hand Hoist
BB-202	Closed Cab with Gravity Feed Dump Body
BB-206	Closed Cab with Mechanical Hoist Type Dump Body
199-A	Closed Cab with Ice Body
BB-330A	Ford School Bus
BB-330B	Ford Passenger Bus
B-76	Open Cab Models
AA-112	Standrive Chassis
315-A	Standrive Delivery

Ford celebrated its 30th Anniversary in 1933 and though their cars featured new designs, frames, and other changes, Ford's trucks saw only minimal changes. One of those changes involved tilting the radiator and its shell back a bit at the top to give these trucks a more aerodynamic look. Another change involved Ford's cataloged Stake and Platform bodies, which this year were widened by 12 inches.

Ford's base engine was again their in-line 4-cylinder, which this year was referred to as a Model C engine. This engine still displaced 200 cubic inches and it was still rated at 50 horsepower, however, it was improved a bit over the 1932 engine. Those improvements included a counterbalanced crankshaft, a bigger water pump, and a revised cylinder head.

The V-8 engine was also improved this year as well with the chief change being the use of higher compression cylinder heads, which boosted the

How do you make a heavy-duty truck out of a 1934 Ford Closed Cab model? You put a heavy-duty frame under it and add a tandem rear axle assembly.

horsepower rating to 75 at 3,800 rpm. Ford trucks powered by V-8 engines this year wore a "V-8" emblem in the middle of their grille towards the topside. All 4-cylinder engine numbers started with a "BB" while the V-8 powered trucks' engine numbers began with "BB18."

The year of 1934 would be the last year that one could buy an Open Cab Ford truck. This would also be the last year that a Ford 4-cylinder engine would be offered in a Ford truck until 1941, when the company would once again offer a 4-cylinder engine in its light-duty trucks. Since this 4-cylinder engine was on its way out this year any changes done to it were minimal, however, major changes were seen on Ford's V-8 engine. Those changes included a cast alloy steel counterbalanced crankshaft that reduced vibrations, redesigned thermostats, a new dual plane intake manifold, new lower compression cast iron cylinder heads, redesigned

valves, open skirted pistons, a new fuel pump, and a new two-barrel carburetor.

All 1934 Ford trucks came equipped with new hoods that featured redesigned hood louvers on their sides. A Ford scripted emblem was mounted in the middle of these louvers. V-8 equipped trucks had a V-8 emblem as part of this trim piece while 4-cylinder equipped trucks had a number "4" cast into their emblems instead of a "V-8."

Ford dropped a number of their specialized bodies from their catalog this year. Gone were the School Bus, the Open Cab Express, and the Heavy-Duty Express. Still, though they offered fewer model choices, Ford had a pretty good sales year considering the fact that they sold about 191,861 trucks in the 1934 model year.

Below you can see the standard models that Ford offered in 1934 and the prices they asked for them:

Here we see a 1934 Ford Closed Cab truck with a Platform Body and a dual rear wheel setup.

Wouldn't you love to ride around in a restored 1934 Ford School Bus like this sharp looking beauty?

Chassis Model	$500
Stake Model (131½-inch wheelbase)	$665
Platform Model (131½-inch wheelbase)	$650
Chassis Model (157-inch wheelbase)	$520
Platform Model (157-inch wheelbase)	$690
Standard Panel (131½-inch wheelbase)	$750
DeLuxe Panel (131½-inch wheelbase)	$780
Stake Model (157-inch wheelbase)	$730
Standard Panel (157-inch wheelbase)	$860

For 1935 Ford promoted its trucks as being "America's Great Truck Value Line" and with good reason. For all the changes that the 1935 Ford trucks underwent the Ford truck buyer of that year "got a lot of bang for his buck."

Let's start with the restyling job that Ford and Budd Manufacturing designers created for these new Ford trucks. Ford called these trucks Model 51s and they featured an all new cab, new front end sheet metal, free standing headlights, partially skirted front fenders, a new grille, and other assorted trim pieces. The new cabs were fitted with safety glass all around, an easy opening windshield to provide ventilation inside the cab, and a comfortable adjustable seat.

The braking system was also improved thanks to a set of larger, cast alloy, ribbed brake drums that cut down on brake fade due to heat.

The only engine now available in a Ford was their 221-cubic-inch V-8 that this year was improved by the use of a new, direct flow crankcase ventilation system. These engines had a tendency to overheat and Ford tried to solve that problem this year by fitting its trucks and cars with larger radiators. Ford also improved the cooling system by putting larger impellers in their water pumps to help circulate coolant faster. A new 19-inch-diameter 4-bladed fan helped too. Cab-Over-Engine trucks were starting to catch on in the trucking business in the mid-1930s but Ford didn't offer such a model in their lineup. That didn't mean that Cab-Over-Engine Ford trucks weren't seen on the streets and the highways and byways of this country. A company called Transportation Engineers, located near Ford headquarters in Michigan, came out with a line of converted Ford trucks they called their "Dearborn Line." To convert one of these Ford trucks they raised the cab mounting and moved it forward. They also fitted these converted Ford Cab-Over-Engine trucks with a new modified hood and modified controls for shifting and steering.

Another company that started modifying Ford trucks in 1935 was Marmon-Herrington. Marmon-Herrington sold a line of their own heavy-duty trucks with All-Wheel-Drive systems but they were looking to increase their business by expanding their line to include lighter-duty trucks. The truck line that they thought would best fit their needs was the V-8 powered Ford. Marmon-Herrington liked the Fords because they were relatively easy to modify and once modified they were the lowest priced All-Wheel-Drive trucks on the market. Marmon-Herrington promoted them as "4 wheel drive trucks at 2 wheel drive prices."

1935 Ford Trucks and Their Prices

131½-inch Wheelbase Chassis $500
131½-inch Wheelbase Chassis with Cab $595
131½-inch Wheelbase Cab with Platform Body
$650
131½-inch Wheelbase Cab with Stake Body $675
131½-inch Wheelbase Panel Truck $760
131½-inch Wheelbase Dump Truck Chassis $530
131½-inch Wheelbase Dump Truck Chassis and
Cab $625
157-inch Wheelbase Dump Truck $800
157-inch Wheelbase Chassis $525
157-inch Wheelbase Chassis and Cab $620
157-inch Wheelbase Cab with Platform Body
$690
157-inch Wheelbase Cab with Stake Body $735

This fine looking 1936 Ford with a stake body was one of the stars of the American Truck Historical Society's National Meet in Kansas City, Missouri, a couple of years ago.

Warner Brothers Studios once owned this beautiful restored 1936 Ford Panel Delivery truck. *Dick Copello Collection*

A rare 1937 "Dearborn Line" Cab-Over-Engine modified Ford truck sits on display at an Ohio truck show some years ago. *Dick Copello Collection*

1938 Ford truck front end details showing grille, hood side vent, Ford emblem, and art deco style radiator ornament.

The year 1936 saw some minor changes made to the looks of the new Ford trucks to help distinguish them from the 1935 models they were replacing. The grille was redesigned along with the radiator cover. The louver treatment on the sides of the hood was also modified. The Ford emblem used on the sides of the hood was moved to the front from the center position it held on the 1935 trucks. Under those hoods could be found a more powerful V-8 engine that was now rated at 80 horsepower.

For school bus manufacturers this year Ford added a new School Bus Chassis to their catalog. In addition to their normal 131½- and 157-inch wheelbases they added a new 191-inch wheelbase for longer bodies like those used on school buses.

Midway through the 1936 model year Ford introduced a new DeLuxe Equipment Package for their truck buyers. This extra cost option included a chrome-plated radiator shell trim piece, a chrome-plated windshield frame, dual horns, a left side exterior rear view mirror, dual wipers, a sun visor, a dome light, a cigarette lighter and ashtray, and a sliding rear cab window.

In May of 1936 the Ford Motor Company hit a milestone with the production of their "3 Millionth Truck." This truck, a 131½-inch wheelbase DeLuxe Panel Delivery, featured special graphics that indicated it was a very special commemorative model. Right after it was produced it was taken on a cross-country promotional tour.

During the 1936 model year Ford came up with a new sales promotional campaign that they dubbed their "On-The-Job-Test." Basically this national campaign by Ford advised potential customers to visit their local Ford dealerships and ask the dealer to loan them a truck so they could put the truck through their own tests to verify whether the said truck could meet all their performance and economy expectations. Did this campaign help to sell more trucks? It probably did but there is no way we can say for sure.

Also during this model year Ford started using testimonial letters from Ford truck owners in their magazine and newspaper advertisements. These letters told how buyers used their trucks and some of them even went so far as to say they regularly overloaded their Ford trucks but that their trucks were more than up to the task without any failures.

Paying For A New Ford Truck

We all know that Henry Ford's primary focus in the automotive business was to provide low cost and dependable cars and trucks to the marketplace. He certainly met that goal but even though his prices were low some people still had problems buying a new Ford vehicle outright, especially during the Great Depression.

For those people Henry Ford offered a solution — buying these vehicles on credit through their dealer network. The Universal Credit Corporation carried these credit contracts. Terms of these contracts included making a down payment and making further payments on a monthly basis. Interest was charged at ½ of 1 percent of the remaining balance per month. Ford even went so far as to advertise credit buying through some of their national promotional campaigns during the 1930s.

Dearborn Line Cab-Over-Engine Fords

These conversions utilized the stock Ford cab, radiator and shell, front fenders, and running boards. These Ford cabs were mounted on a platform that was about 1½ feet in height. Besides being mounted higher these cabs were moved forward by 2¼ feet, which put the cowl hood line in the middle of the front fenders. The Transportation Engineers Company that did these conversions provided them with a special shortened hood, mounting platform, separation panels, a modified steering kit, and other assorted parts and pieces to make this conversion work.

You might ask why a truck buyer would go to all

Another shot of a 1938 Ford Cab-Over-Engine truck with a tow truck service body.

this trouble and extra cost for a truck? The answer is pretty simple. These trucks had a shorter back-of-cab-to-front-axle length, which allowed the use of a longer body and increased load capacity. This translated into more cargo being transported, less trips to make, and lower associated costs, which meant more profit for the business. Another added bonus that Cab-Over-Engine trucks provided was that they were easier to maneuver in the tighter confines of city deliveries.

For years critics of Ford trucks claimed that they were not the most economical trucks to own because of their use of V-8 engines in a day and age when the competition was using 4- and 6-cylinder engines. In response to those criticisms in 1937 Ford offered their car and truck buyers a choice of two engines. For those who wanted more power Ford offered a more powerful V-8 engine that was rated at 85 horsepower. This engine was called the V-8 85. For lighter-duty work, or for buyers who wanted more economy and less power,

Look at the sides of this 1938 Ford truck hood. Note the oval Ford hood emblem with the number 85 embossed on the bottom of it, meaning this truck was originally powered by an 85 horsepower Ford V-8 engine.

Ford's new engine was a smaller 136-cubic-inch V-8 that carried a rating of 60 horsepower. Because of that horsepower rating this engine came to be known as the V-8 60. This engine was offered in Ford cars, Commercial Cars, and 131½-inch wheelbase trucks. In most cases these engines were overworked when used in trucks so their economical gains as compared to the higher rated V-8 Ford engines were minimal to say the least.

Ford V-8 85 engines still displaced 221 cubic inches but they were revised this year to feature a number of improvements including a reworked cylinder block, cast steel pistons, cast iron heads, and integrated, self lubricated water pumps.

Ford heavily promoted their "Engine Exchange Plan" in all their truck ads this year. This plan allowed a buyer to replace a worn out engine with a factory-rebuilt unit at a lower cost than what a local rebuilding shop would charge.

In addition to offering a new V-8 engine Ford trucks of 1937 featured a new grille design and a new grille surround, along with a new louver design

on its hood sides. Another distinctive feature on these trucks was their new, two-piece, V-type windshield design. In order to accommodate that new two-piece windshield the Ford cabs had a modified roof panel, a modified dashboard panel, a modified cowl, and a modified hood.

During the 1937 model year Ford also introduced a new 141-inch wheelbase Transit Bus Chassis. This bus chassis utilized an 85-hp Ford V-8 engine in a forward control chassis where the driver sits beside the engine. These buses accommodated 25 passengers and used a 12-volt electrical system.

Ford trucks were completely redesigned for the 1938 model year. These trucks featured a redesigned cab with more rounded corners, a new hood that opened from the front rather than the side, new fenders, new headlights, and new exterior trim pieces. The most controversial aspect of this new design was its large oval-shaped grille. Some people said that grille "looked like a pair of lips sucking on a lemon."

These trucks were once again offered as Standard or DeLuxe models. The extra cost DeLuxe models used a chrome-plated grille, a chrome-plated windshield frame, a hinge-mounted exterior mirror, and wheels that were color-coordinated to the body color.

Bowing to popular demand, in May of 1938 the Ford Motor Company introduced their first Cab-Over-Engine (COE) models. These trucks used a regular cab that was widened by about 7½ inches and these same cabs were raised by 7½ inches and moved forward on the chassis to provide for engine clearance. Ford's COE trucks also used a special front axle that was mounted on a set of parallel leaf springs rather than a single transverse type spring and front axle arrangement used on Ford's conventional trucks. Two wheelbase lengths were offered with these Ford COE trucks: a short 101-inch wheelbase and a longer 134-inch wheelbase.

Because of the addition of COE models to

their catalog Ford started referring to their conventional cab trucks as "Regulars." The wheelbase on base model Regulars this year was increased from 131½ inches to 134. These new chassis also featured improved brakes, heavier-duty springs and axles, and an improved steering system.

The only engine offered in Regular or COE Ford trucks this year was the 221-cubic-inch 85-hp V-8. The smaller 60-hp V-8 was restricted to use in Ford cars and their light-duty Commercial Car vehicles. The 85-hp V-8 had a redesigned cylinder head this year, which incorporated the use of 24 retaining studs rather than the 21 studs used previously for better seating.

About the same time Ford introduced their COE trucks they also offered a new, vacuum operated 2-speed rear axle as an option for economy minded truck buyers. A dashboard-mounted lever control doubled the amount of forward gears to eight and reverse gears to two. With that many gears to choose from a driver could select his gears for maximum efficiency and economy depending on his load, his road speed, and whether he was operating in the slow confines of the city or whether he was driving on the open road between cities or towns.

The biggest news concerning Ford vehicles in 1939 was Henry Ford's adoption of hydraulic braking systems on all his cars and trucks. Henry had lagged behind the competition that had switched over to hydraulics earlier in the decade. These brakes were now more efficient in their operation thanks to an equal amount of pressure being used on all four corners of the vehicle. Mechanical brakes were fine in the earlier days of the automobile as long as they were adjusted properly. However, the days of mechanical brakes were over long before Henry Ford made the switch.

Ford also took the opportunity to introduce a new automobile to its stable in 1939. It was called the Mercury and one of its features over the regular Fords was its use of a new 239-cubic-inch Flat-

Check out that oval grille. It was quite a conversation piece when it was first shown on 1938 Ford trucks. The example shown here is a 1939 DeLuxe model.

head V-8 that was rated at 95 horsepower. As an added bonus this new Mercury V-8 could also be had as an optional Ford truck engine for an extra $25. Of course, in the Ford truck it was called a Ford V-8, but nevertheless it was the same engine. In any event an extra 10 horsepower for only $25 was quite a bargain especially to a truck buyer who needed more power.

That brings us to the end of this decade and we can see that it was a good decade as far as the Ford Motor Company was concerned. During this time Ford introduced a number of new stylish models that were better equipped than Ford cars and trucks of an earlier time. They had more powerful engines, heavier-duty frames, springs, and axles. And let us not forget the brakes and improvements done to other systems. These improvements came about because customers demanded them and in order for Ford to successfully compete in these highly competitive times they had to give the customer what he or she wanted. Some automobile and truck companies didn't offer these improvements and unfortunately they didn't survive past this decade.

This beautifully restored Ford Cab-Over-Engine truck is a 1940 model. It was photographed in May of 2004 at a truck show in California.

Chapter 4: Pre- and Post-War Years For Ford 1940-1947

The year of 1940 saw some major changes to Ford's truck lineup. First and foremost the torque tube type rear end on all trucks above a ½-ton rating was replaced by a new Hotchkiss type rear axle setup using a separate driveshaft between the transmission and rear axle.

In addition to coming up with a new rear axle setup for these trucks Ford also redesigned the front axle and spring setups. Instead of having the front axle suspended with one transverse mounted spring like before these new Fords had their front axle mounted to a set of parallel front leaf springs, a setup that was found on Ford's 1938 and 1939 COE trucks.

Changing the front end and rear end setups on these trucks required that their frames had to be re-engineered as well, which Ford did. They also beefed up the frames for higher loads by increasing spring strengths.

Besides changing what was found on the underside of their trucks Ford also took the opportunity to freshen up the looks of their 1940 vehicles by redesigning cabs, fenders, hoods, and trim pieces as well. The cabs on Ford's Regular truck models were treated to a new upper body stamping that included the roof panel, cowl, and windshield surround in a single piece rather than in multiple pieces as on previous cabs. The dashboards in these cabs were also reworked so that they would fit better with the changes.

These new Regular Ford trucks came with new hoods, new headlights, new trim pieces, and a new, more subdued grille treatment that was a lot less controversial than the grille used in 1938 and 1939 models. The new hoods on these models used a new design of louvers on their sides and towards the front of the hood a "V-8" symbol was embossed in the metal. Another change was seen in the bull nose trim piece that sat on the front of the nose. In this trim piece the horsepower figure of the engine was embossed. The 85-hp V-8 engine had an "85" on this piece while the 95-hp engine had a "95" cast into this trim piece.

In marked contrast to all the changes seen on the Regular Ford truck models the only real changes seen on the Cab-Over-Engine Ford trucks were a different grille design and an emblem sitting above the grille. The cabs they used were still the same as the cabs used in 1938 and 1939.

In 1941, for the first time in 33 years, Ford added an in-line 6-cylinder engine to his car and truck lineups. Practically all of these new 6-cylinder engines were used in cars but some found their way into trucks. This new 6-cylinder engine displaced 226 cubic inches and was rated at 90 horsepower (the same as the 221-cubic-inch V-8). Its maximum torque rating of 180 ft/lbs was rated higher than the torque rating for the V-8, which made it perfect for truck use. Ford also offered a 4-cylinder engine in their pickup truck models this year in addition to their regular V-8 and 6-cylinder engines.

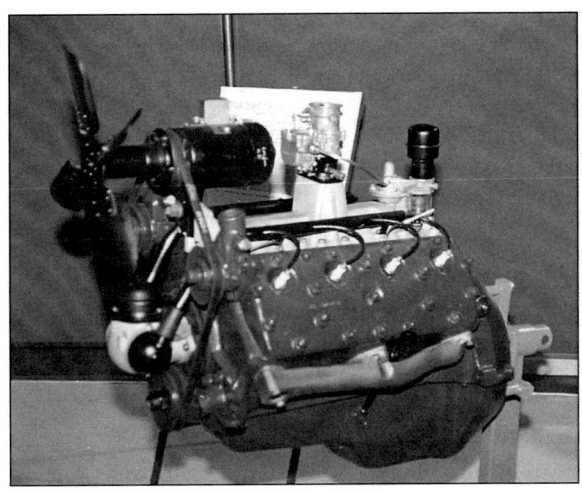

On this engine stand a Flathead Ford V-8 is displayed.

This bull nose molding was used on 1940 Ford truck hoods. You can't see it well in this photograph but at the top of this molding the number "95" is cast, indicating it is equipped with the optional 95-horsepower engine that was offered for Ford trucks in 1940.

Here we see a close up shot of a 1940 Ford grille. It is still in remarkable original condition even though it is over 64 years old.

In this shot we can see the extruded stylized V-8 emblem that appeared on the sides of 1940 Ford hoods.

Since Ford offered other engine choices this year the embossed, stylized "V-8" emblem that appeared on the sides of the hoods used on their Regular trucks was gone. The hood side louver treatment was also changed on 1941 Fords and a wider bull nose molding and hood trim were also featured on these new Fords.

Ford's Cab-Over-Engine trucks still used the 1938 style cab this year but the hood and grille on these trucks were modified to make them look more like the grille used on Ford's Regular truck models. These COE models also used modified dashboards and other trim changes in their interiors as well.

The 1942 model year brought a number of major changes to Ford cars and trucks. For their Regular and COE trucks Ford used carryover cabs and the front ends found on the conventional or Regular Ford trucks were restyled. This restyling job included a new hood design, new front fenders, new grilles, new headlights, new bumpers, and new trim pieces. These changes made the 1942 Ford trucks look a lot different than the 1941 trucks they replaced.

This new model year had barely begun when the Japanese attacked Pearl Harbor forcing the United States into fighting in World War II. Because of war demands on products production of cars and trucks for normal civilian use came to a stop in early February 1942 so the automobile manufacturers could concentrate all their efforts into producing goods to help us win the war.

Though civilian production of vehicles was stopped Ford still produced military trucks during 1943 and 1944. These conventional Ford trucks looked like civilian versions of 1942 models except for their military equipment and markings. In addition to these regular conventional trucks Ford also produced thousands of 4-wheel-drive jeep type vehicles for military use during this time. They also produced some special military 4x4 vehicles that were rated at 1½ tons. Ford started building these trucks in 1944 and referred to them as "GTP" models. These special trucks were built on a forward control chassis layout and were powered by Ford 6-cylinder engines.

Also during 1944, probably around the middle of the year, the automobile manufacturers were allowed to produce some medium- and heavy-duty trucks for civilian use to replace trucks that were starting to break down. For Ford this meant starting to produce their 1942 conventional models, but in order to buy one you had to show proof that you were on an approved list for companies involved in providing vital services. As we said, these were basically carryover 1942 models that were placed on heavier-duty frames and used bigger gas tanks, black-out style headlamps, and other modifications.

In early May of 1945 the automobile manufacturers were given the okay to start limited production of vehicles for the civilian market by the War Production Board. In trucks these vehicles were mostly light-duty models like pickups, which were joined by the heavier-duty models approved previously. Now one didn't need to be on an "approved" list to buy one but because of pent-up demand long waiting lists were the norm. At first the only engine available in these Ford trucks was the 239-cubic-inch V-8 now rated at 100 horsepower but after a while the 226-cubic-inch 6-cylinder engine became available. The 221-cubic-inch V-8 engine and the Ford 4-cylinder engine were no longer available for these Fords.

For the 1946 model year, which started in late 1945, very little had changed in the looks of the Ford truck line. It was hard to tell the differences in these trucks from what was offered back in 1942.

Once again these trucks were available with either a 6-cylinder engine or a V-8. When equipped with a V-8 they carried model numbers that started with a "69T" (134-inch wheelbase) or a "698T" (158-inch wheelbase), or if they came with a 6-cylinder engine their model numbers were "6GT"

Here is the "Baumis Manufacturing" that appeared on the sides of Ford trucks that featured one of their tandem rear axle setups.

A close up view of a 1941 Ford truck bull nose hood ornament. It has an art deco look to it.

Here is another photo of one of Hess Motor Service's 1941 Ford tow trucks done up in a two-tone paint finish. *Charles Hess Collection*

This photograph shows the other Hess Motor Service 1941 Ford tow truck that is a common sight on the streets of Wadena, Minnesota. *Charles Hess Collection*

(134-inch wheelbase) or "6G8T" for a truck with a 158-inch wheelbase.

This year Ford also offered Heavy-Duty versions of these same trucks, which incidentally carried the same designations. The heavier-duty rated trucks used 2-speed rear axles, larger tires, stiffer springs, vacuum assisted brakes, and beefed-up frames to carry heavier loads. When equipped as such these trucks carried a nominal rating of 2½ tons.

Besides being built here in the United States over the years Ford trucks have been built in other countries. Some of these foreign built Ford trucks bear a likeness to Ford trucks built here while others tended to look different due mostly to laws governing engines, sizes, wheelbases, tonnage ratings, and local content statutes. The country producing the greatest number of look alike Ford trucks is Canada. Canadian built Ford trucks look just like their USA built counterparts.

In 1946 Ford of Canada decided to augment their Ford truck production by releasing a new line of Mercury trucks. The main reason why they took this step was to appease Mercury dealers who wanted to sell a truck of their own. Basically the Mercury line of Canadian built trucks looked just like their Ford trucks except for Mercury trim items like grilles, model designations, and unique trim pieces. Canadian built Mercury trucks have always been rare and are even more rare today.

After being missed in the 1945 model year Ford's Cab-Over-Engine trucks made a return appearance to the Ford truck lineup for the 1946 model year. When placed on a 101-inch wheelbase chassis these trucks carried a model number that began with "691." 134-inch wheelbase models and 158-inch wheelbase models had model numbers that started with "69W" or "698W" (158) respectively. These trucks still used the 1938 style cab and the hood and grille changes that were noted on the 1941 models before the United States entered World War II.

For all intents and purposes the 1947 Ford truck models were the same as what was offered in 1946 except for the model year designation and some model codes.

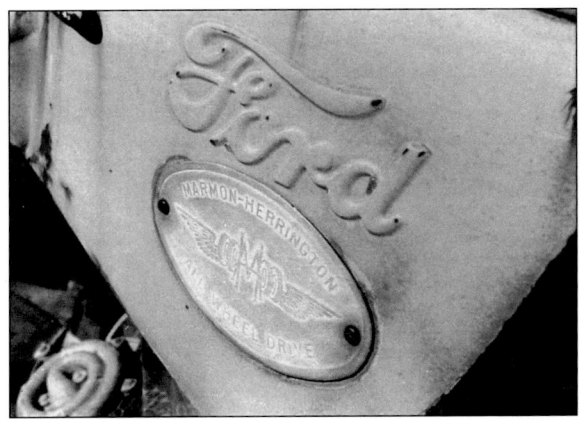

Marmon-Herrington tag as used on 1940s Ford modified trucks. These tags were mounted on the sides of the hood near the cowl.

Ford produced a number of these GTP trucks for the war effort in 1943 and 1944. This particular truck has been outfitted as a troop carrier.

Stenciled on the back of the seats in these Ford GTP vehicles you can see Ford Motor Company information.

Another Ford GTP vehicle with a front-mounted winch and a fold-down windshield.

Close up view of the interiors found in Ford GTP vehicles. Pretty spartan, huh?

A Ford GTP vehicle set up as a dump truck for construction work.

A close up view of a 1943-1944 Ford GTP vehicle. These trucks used military spec tires, heavy-duty winches, tow hooks, and other military hardware.

39

A new Ford Cab-Over-Engine truck pulls a trailer full of new Fords to a new car dealer in 1946. *Dick Copello Collection*

This 1942 Ford Texaco tanker looks just like the gasoline tanker that appeared in one of Ford's 1946 truck ads.

Close up view of Ford script and trim used on Ford truck hoods from the 1940s.

This restored Ford truck just happens to be a 1942 model. These 1942 Ford trucks were a rare sight back in 1942 and are even more so today.

The owner of this restored 1947 Ford truck is so proud of it he displays his truck at truck shows with this custom signboard.

This is one sharp looking restored Ford truck from the 1940s. Wouldn't you like to have one of these for your own?

41

This Ford promotional photograph taken in the late 1940s shows a prototype Ford F-5 Stake truck. *Ford Motor Company Photograph*

Chapter 5: F Series and Bonus Built Trucks Leading the Way 1948-1952

On January 16, 1948, the most popular and longest running line of Ford trucks made their debut, for on this date the F Series Ford truck was born. This new line of Ford trucks ranged in size from the light-duty ½-ton rated F-1 pickup to the Extra Heavy-Duty, 3-ton rated F-8. All totaled there were over 100 different cab, body, and chassis configurations that comprised this new series of Ford trucks.

Ford referred to these trucks as their "Bonus Built" models in all their promotional materials that were prepared and distributed during this era.

In 1948 all Ford trucks featured totally restyled cabs, fenders, doors, hoods, grilles, and the like. The cabs were a bit wider than those previously used and were a lot more comfortable and roomy. They also featured a one-piece windshield again, the first one since 1936. Vent windows in the doors helped to circulate air through the cab, which was really appreciated on warm days.

Both conventional and Cab-Over-Engine models shared these cabs. The Cab-Over-Engine models had their cabs mounted further back on their frames now so they didn't need to use a special cab that was different than the cab used on conventional trucks. Though they used the same cabs the Cab-Over-Engine models had their own unique doors, hoods, and front fenders. Since these cabs sat higher on the frames than the conventional truck models fender mounted steps were provided to help the driver and passengers to enter or exit the cab with ease. The step on the right side also served double duty as a covered battery box.

Since these COE cabs were mounted further back on the chassis than earlier models the wheelbase on the shortest COE chassis was stretched out from 101 to 110 inches. These trucks were also available again with 134- and 158-inch wheelbases.

These Cab-Over-Engine trucks were available in Ford's Medium-Duty range as F-5 and F-6 models and they could be had with either 6-cylinder or V-8 engines. Prior to 1948 all Ford COE trucks were only available with V-8 engines. When powered by a 6-cylinder engine these trucks carried a model code that started with a "7H" while the V-8 model code started with an "8R." The 6-cylinder engine had been improved a bit starting in 1947 and the 1948 year would see a number of improvements done to the V-8 Ford truck engine. Both still displaced 226 and 239 cubic inches, respectively, but the V-8, now called the "Rouge 239," used a different block, cylinder heads, crankshaft, and other internal parts and pieces.

Though it wasn't well known at that time, or since then for that matter, some Ford Medium-Duty, Heavy-Duty, and Extra Heavy-Duty trucks of this period were offered with diesel engines for export markets. As far as we know none of these "Bonus Built" diesel powered trucks were offered for sale in the North American market.

1949 was basically the "Year of the Car" at the Ford Motor Company with new models of Fords, Mercurys, and Lincolns being released. Very little funding was given over to refining Ford's truck lineup for this year. However, some changes were incorporated which increased the number of available F Series models from 139 at the beginning of the model year to around 160 by mid year.

One of those changes, a major one at that, involved the addition of a new 176-inch-long wheel-

This photo shows the combination battery box and side step used on the right side running board of Ford COE trucks.

base chassis for Ford Medium-Duty F-5 and F-6 trucks. Another change involved Ford's F-4 models, which when equipped with dual rear tires and placed on a 134-inch wheelbase chassis with heavier-duty springs, was considered to be the lightest Medium-Duty Ford truck offered in their 1949 catalog. Gone this year was the standard 2-speed rear axle that was offered on the F-6 and F-8. The standard rear axle for these trucks was now a single speed unit, however, for those truck buyers who still wanted a 2-speed rear axle, one was available as an extra cost option.

Though the "Bonus Built" Ford trucks of 1950 looked like the 1948 and 1949 models that

Doesn't this truck look cute? It is a 1948 Ford F-5 done up with dual exhaust stacks, West Coast mirrors, and a set of rear fenders.

Hood side trim used on 1948-'50 Ford F Series trucks.

preceded them Ford did make some changes to improve these trucks. Chief among those changes were higher GVW ratings and a new "Big Six" engine option for the F-6 line of trucks. This engine formerly used in Ford's Transit Bus Program displaced 254 cubic inches and had a maximum gross horsepower rating of 110 at 3,400 rpm. Compare that figure to the "Rouge 226" (6 cylinder), which

had a gross horsepower figure of 95 at 3,300 rpm and the "Rouge 239" (V-8) whose gross horsepower figure was 100 at 3,800 rpm. Besides a higher horsepower figure the "Rouge 254 Big Six" engine had a gross maximum torque figure of 212 ft/lbs at 1,200 rpm. This figure was a good 32 ft/lbs higher than what was offered on the other engines at the same low RPM rate. In other words, this engine offered more "grunt" or pulling power in the low ranges, which was very important to a truck buyer who was looking for the economy of a 6-cylinder engine with more power and torque on tap than a V-8 engine could offer.

For those wanting a large van type delivery vehicle in a medium-duty truck range this year Ford offered two F-5 Parcel Delivery units. One was put on a 134-inch wheelbase while the other was offered on a 158-inch wheelbase chassis. Both came with 226 cubic inch "Rouge 226" 6-cylinder engines with 3-speed manual transmissions as standard equipment. These trucks were similar to the UPS trucks we see today.

Towards the end of the 1950 model year the "Bonus Built" Ford trucks were starting to look a bit dated and for good reason. Except for some minor trim and appearance changes the 1950 models looked like the 1948 and 1949 trucks that preceded them. It was hard to tell the three of them apart from each other. But that all changed when truck buyers got their first look at Ford's restyled 1951 "Bonus Built" F Series trucks.

This restyling job, a major one at that, included a new grille, new headlight treatments, a restyled hood, a cab with a larger rear window, and restyled exterior trim pieces. Rather than using a set of horizontal bars for a grille, as was done on the 1948-50 Ford F Series trucks, the new grille treatment seen on these trucks combined a thick horizontal bar that ran between the two headlight pods that was supported by three short vertical bars with three orb-like spheres. This new grille was then placed in a larger, wider grille opening. To accomplish this change Ford also did a major modifying job on the front fenders.

On top of those revamped front fenders these new "Bonus Built" Fords used a restyled hood with changes seen in the front area around the air intake, the side vent area, and respective trim pieces that were used to highlight these areas.

For the first time in many years the Ford truck buyer in 1951 was afforded the choice of a standard cab or a more deluxe equipped version. Ford called the former a "Five Star Cab" while the latter was called a "Five Star Extra Cab." Of course, the "Five Star Extra Cab" cost a bit more but for that extra cost buyers got a much better truck.

Five Star Extra Cab Equipment
Foam Rubber Padding in Seat
Thermacoustic Headlining Cover
1½-Inch Glass Wool Insulated Roof Pad
Chrome-Plated Windshield Molding
Bright Finished Metal Vent Window Frames
Two-Tone Upholstery
Special Door and Body Interior Panels
Dual Sun Visors
Dual Armrests on Doors
Illuminated Cigar Lighter
Locking Glove Box
Locks on Both Doors
Dual Matched Tone Electric Horns
Dome Light with Door Frame Mounted Switches

The major changes seen on Ford's 1952 models were seen under the hood rather than on the outside of these trucks. For this year a more modern, overhead valve engine that displaced 215 cubic inches replaced Ford's L Head Flathead in-line 6-cylinder engine called the "Rouge 226." Though this engine was smaller in size it still put out more horsepower and attained better fuel economy than the old 226 it replaced. Ford called this new engine their "Cost Clipper Six" and its maximum, or gross, horsepower rating was now listed at 101 at 3,500 rpm.

Hood side trim as used on 1948-'50 Ford Cab-Over-Engine trucks.

Besides this new engine the 1952 Ford truck buyers saw some changes in exterior trim pieces, which helped to distinguish these new trucks from the models they replaced.

Though this period in Ford truck history lasted less than five years the effect of Ford's "Bonus Built" trucks was felt throughout the marketplace. The 1940s era Ford trucks that preceded them were popular trucks in their own right but the "Bonus Built" Fords were even more popular and some say that they had a hand in saving the company from going under. At the time that these trucks first appeared on the drawing boards the Ford Motor Company was in dire straits and the engineers, designers, and marketing people who witnessed their development knew that they had to build a series of trucks that would raise the bar for all involved in the trucking business. Giving something extra to the customer was the goal and Ford did just that when they introduced their "Bonus Built" trucks in January 1948.

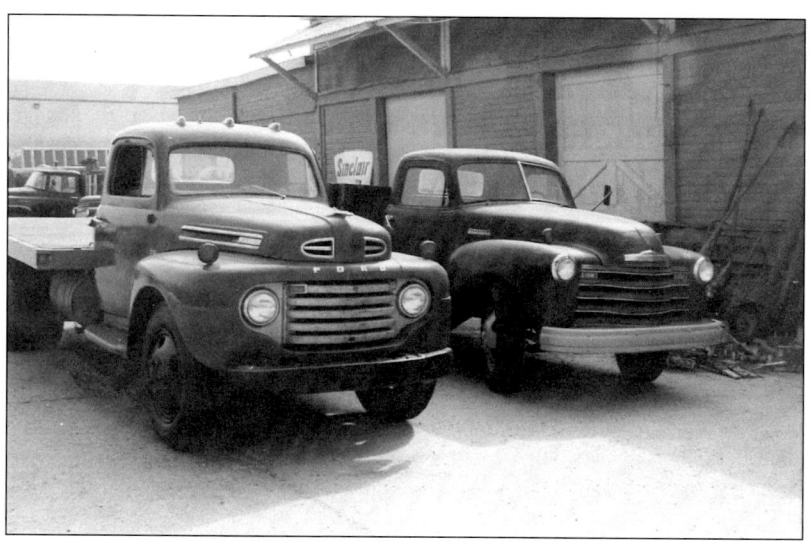

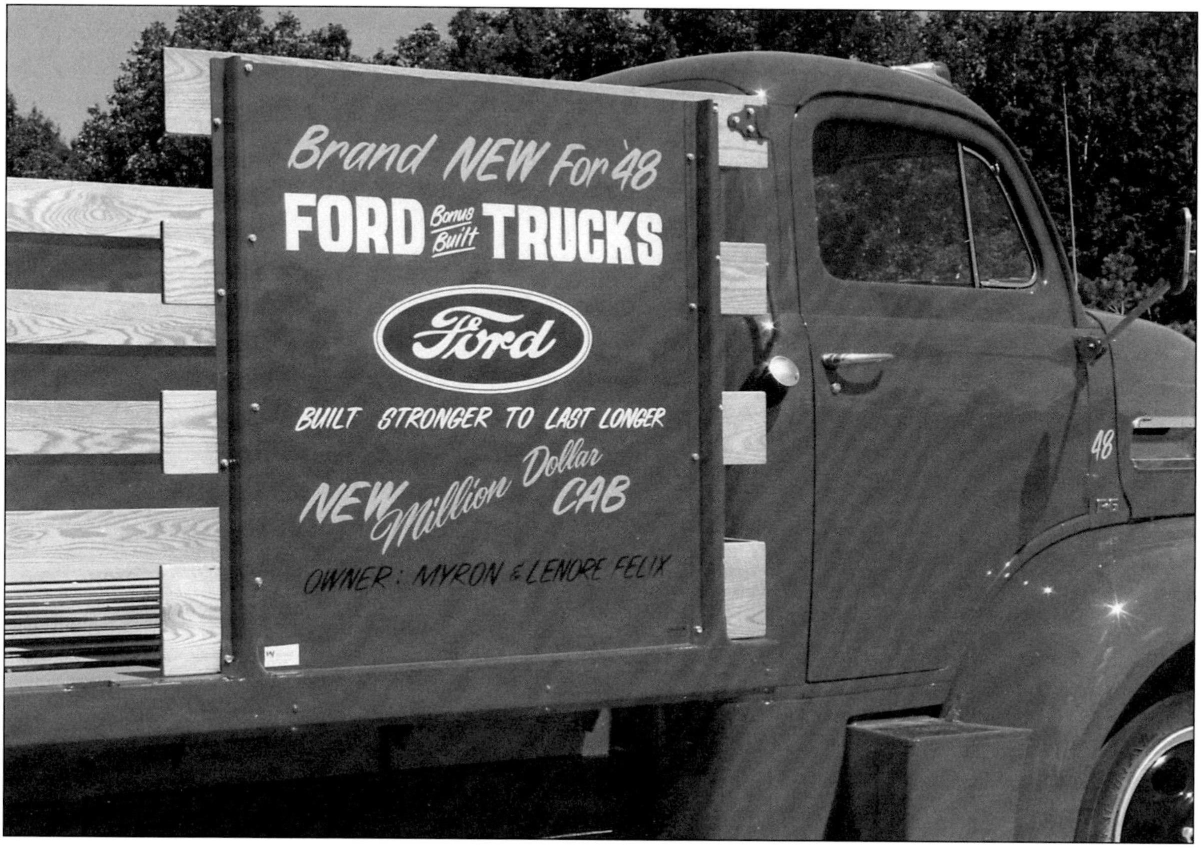
Brand NEW For '48
FORD Bonus Built TRUCKS
Ford
BUILT STRONGER TO LAST LONGER
NEW Million Dollar CAB
OWNER: MYRON & LENORE FELIX
48

If you want to dress up the sides of your Ford truck do what Myron Felix did. Have some custom promotional signs made up for it just like the signs that Ford dealers used years ago.

Sinclair

A Ford "Bonus Built" 1948-'50 truck displayed beside one of its biggest competitors on a truck lot in Kansas back in the 1990s.

A Ford tractor-trailer rig hauls some new Ford sedans in California back in 1949. *Dick Copello Collection*

A young man seeks some shade coverage under a 1949 Ford COE Platform truck in New Mexico. It is done up in an Army motif.

This 1949 Ford truck with stainless steel grille bars was seen at a truck show in California back in the late 1980s.

This beautifully restored 1950 Ford Stake truck hails from Minnesota.

Somebody has added a 1953 or later Ford crest to the front of this 1948-'50 truck hood.

Looking for a cool rig to haul your collectible cars and trucks to shows? How about using a neat looking Ford COE truck like the one shown here.

Interior shot of a 1951 Ford F Series truck focusing on the instruments.

Grille, hood, and front end trim details used on a 1951 Ford F Series truck with a 6-cylinder engine.

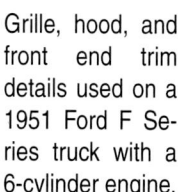

Here is a photograph of a very rare truck. A 1952 Ford F-5 outfitted with a Marmon-Herrington "All-Wheel-Drive" conversion.

Marmon-Herrington "All-Wheel-Drive" badge that was affixed to the hoods of converted Ford trucks.

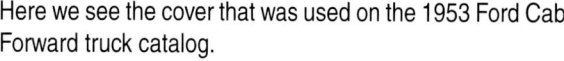

Here we see the cover that was used on the 1953 Ford Cab Forward truck catalog.

This is the new Ford truck crest emblem that started appearing on Ford trucks with their 1953 models.

Chapter 6: A New Look Along With New Model Numbers 1953-1956

The Ford Motor Company reached a milestone in 1953 when they reached their "Golden Anniversary" year. The company celebrated this special event by introducing a redesigned lineup of truck vehicles. Besides their new looks these trucks also received new model designations. The F-1 became the F-100, the F-2 became the F-250, the F-3 became the F-350, and so on. Ford's Medium-Duty Trucks, previously called the F-5 and F-6, were now called the F-500 and F-600.

The School Bus Chassis models in the medium-duty range were now referred to as the B-500 and B-600 and the Parcel Delivery trucks became Ford's P Series. Ford's Cab-Over-Engine trucks, which were part of the F Series line before, now had their own series designation. They were now referred to as "Cab Forward" trucks under the "C" Series.

Ford referred to their previous series of trucks as being their "Bonus Built Line" while these new

Fords were called their "Economy Trucks." Ford used this promotional term to describe this line of trucks because they said they were economical to run, economical in time savings, and economical to own.

Ford's main focus this year revolved around their new cabs, which they termed as being "Driverized." They were designed from the start to provide a comfortable environment for the driver and passengers. It is said that Ford used mannequins to design the seats and to locate all the instruments and controls within easy reach of the driver. They may not have known it at the time but those Ford designers and engineers were probably the first of their kind to use ergonomics to design the interior of a truck. The cabs were wider by five inches or so over the cabs that were used in the "Bonus Built" trucks that they replaced. Besides being wider these cabs featured more leg and hip room for more comfort. Wider door openings allowed for easier entry and exit into and out of these cabs and a larger windshield and rear window made it easier to see into and out of these new cabs.

The most prominent feature on these restyled Ford trucks were their front fenders, which were now wider and a bit larger than the fenders seen on earlier Ford trucks. These fenders were joined by a new hood, which was also larger, wider, and flatter than previous F Series truck hoods. On the front of this restyled hood Ford used a new truck crest trim emblem which had a similar shape to the hood emblem used on their cars. However, the truck crest used a different design in its center. This design featured a gear bisected by a lightning bolt. A new grille and exterior trim pieces helped to further set these trucks apart from what came before.

Underneath all this new sheet metal Ford used a new sturdier frame for support. On the front of the frames one could see a new set back front axle. When combined with a new steering system the turning radiuses of these trucks were shortened quite a bit making them easier to maneuver in all types of driving situations. Longer springs

In this Ford Motor Company promotional photograph we can see what a Ford F Series cab looked like between 1953 and 1955. *Ford Motor Company Photograph*

on the front and rear axles gave a better ride. And a wider tread made these trucks more stable than earlier models.

The engines for these new "Economy Trucks" were the same as what was offered the previous year but the manual transmissions offered as standard equipment now had synchronizers on all forward gears so that a driver didn't have to double clutch anymore to change gears smoothly.

Once again Ford offered these trucks in standard or deluxe versions. Ford referred to the standard issue truck as a "Driverized Cab Standard" while the extra cost deluxe version was called a "Ford Driverized DeLuxe Cab."

A 1954 Marmon-Herrington Ford F-600 "All-Wheel-Drive" truck is shown working in a baseball field in this photograph. *Bill Fox Collection*

We found this 1954 Ford Cab Forward C-600 sitting in the middle of a field near Williams, Arizona.

1953 Ford Driverized DeLuxe Cab Equipment

Spear Ornaments on Hood Sides
Bright Metal Trim Bars to Accentuate the Grille
Chromed Vent Window Frames
Dual Matching Tone Electric Horns
Two-Tone Seat Upholstery
DeLuxe Interior Door Trim Panels
Perforated Thermacoustic Headliner Covering
Glass Wool Insulation Pad Underside of Roof Panel
Foam Rubber Seat Padding
Sound Deadener on Floor and Rear Cab Panels
Dual Sun Visors
Dual Armrests
Illuminated Cigar Lighter
Dome Light with Door Frame Mounted Switches
Locks on Both Doors
Sturdy Lock on Dispatch Box (Glove Box)
Rubber Floor Mat

This 1954 Ford C-600 Cab Forward Platform truck is powered by a V-8 engine and features deluxe trim pieces.

For 1954 Ford trucks didn't look any different from the outside except for grille design changes and changes in the designs of exterior trim pieces.

After a 21-year run Ford stopped putting their venerable L Head, affectionately known as the "Flathead V-8," in the cars and trucks they built here in the USA. Those engines were replaced with a modern, large bore, small stroke, overhead valve V-8 engine. Ford referred to these engines as their "Y Block" V-8s because the sides of the block casting ran down below the center of the crankshaft making the engine look like a letter "Y" from the front. By designing the engine in this fashion Ford strengthened the bottom of the block while at the same time supported the crankshaft better making for a stouter, more durable engine.

In their Medium-Duty Line Ford offered two of these new engines, which they called "Power King V-8s." The first engine displaced 239 cubic inches, the same cubic inch size as the Flathead engine it replaced. However, this new engine was rated at 130 horsepower at 4,200 rpm and had a gross, or maximum, torque rating of 214 ft/lbs at 1,800 to 2,200 rpm. This engine was an extra cost option for an F-500 model but it was standard equipment for an F-600. The standard engine for the F-500, B-500, and P-500 was a new 223 cubic inch "Cost Clipper Six." This new 6-cylinder engine carried a maximum horsepower rating of 115 at 3,900 rpm and a maximum torque rating of 193 ft/lbs between 1,800 and 2,200 rpm. If you wanted a little more horsepower for your F-600 truck there was another "Power King V-8" optional engine you could choose.

This version had a cubic inch displacement of 256 cubic inches and had a maximum horsepower

Front end grille and trim details on a 1955 Ford F Series truck. The "stylized" star design in the middle indicates that this truck originally came with a 6-cylinder engine.

rating of 138 at 3,900 rpm. It was also a torquier engine with a gross rating of 226 ft/lbs between 1,900 and 2,400 rpm.

Like the 1954 models that came before them the 1955 Ford trucks featured a new grille treatment and redesigned exterior trim pieces. The new grille design featured a two horizontal bar motif. The upper bar formed a "V" while the lower bar was straight. Both bars extended from one headlight pod to the other. In the center of the "V" in the upper bar was either a stylized star emblem or a V-8 emblem. The V-8 emblem indicated that a V-8 engine powered the truck while the star meant there was a 6-cylinder engine sitting under the hood.

Once again Ford offered their truck buyers the choice between a standard model and a deluxe version. But instead of calling the fancier model a "DeLuxe," this year they called it a "Custom Cab." And like the fancier models offered before this Custom Cab option came with

This photo shows a 1955 Ford F-500 truck that has been fitted with a farm body. The bright grille trim and cab roof trim band identify it as a Custom Cab model.

A 1955 Ford F-500 dump truck is shown in this photograph. It was offered up for bids at an auction during the American Truck Historical Society's National Meet in Fontana, California, in May of 2004.

lots of deluxe equipment — two-tone deluxe upholstery, chrome-plated dress up trim, dual horns, dual sun visors, extra padding and sound insulation, and, of course, "Custom Cab" identification emblems. This year Ford also began offering truck buyers a two-tone exterior paint treatment. This two-tone option had Ford painting the roof white with the rest of the cab, fenders, hood, and body painted in a complementary shade of paint. This option, when combined with the "Custom Cab" option, provided for one sharp looking truck.

Chevrolet upped the ante in the truck sales wars with their release of a new restyled truck line halfway through the 1955 model year. Next to these redesigned Chevrolets Ford's "Economy Trucks" looked a bit dated. Ford would have liked to come out with a restyled truck of its own and they had one on the drawing boards but it wasn't ready for production yet. So Ford's designers and body engineers came up with an interim solution to help

handle this situation. They would take their current cab and modify its cowl panel, doors, windshield, and roof panel to accept a new wraparound windshield. The end result was a new look and one that would make the 1956 Ford truck one of the most popular Ford trucks of all time.

Ford's truck lineup for 1956 comprised over 280 different models — trucks to handle just about any trucking job imaginable.

Besides a new look these new Fords received improved electrical and ignition systems when Ford made the upgrade from 6- to 12-volt electrical systems for their cars and trucks. Besides the cab design changes these new Fords came with a redesigned grille and hood trim pieces. And on the "Custom Cab" models Ford offered an item that hadn't been seen on a Ford truck since the late 1930s. This item was a chrome-plated grille that really dressed up the exterior looks of these trucks. This chrome-plated grille was part of the standard

This 1955 Ford F-500 Platform Body truck looks really sharp with its chrome mirrors and Custom Cab trim.

This "Custom Cab" emblem was mounted to the upper door area on 1956 Ford trucks that were equipped with this option.

equipment offered with the "Custom Cab" package. It was also available as an extra cost option on standard model trucks as well. Quite a few of these standard model 1956 Ford trucks were dressed up with the addition of this special grille.

This year Ford also increased the cubic inch displacements of their "Power King" V-8 engines. Gone were the 239 and 256 cubic inch versions and in their place were three 272 cubic inch V-8s with horsepower ratings of 158, 167, and 168.

Another option that came on line for these 1956 Ford trucks was a "Big Back Window Option." This option provided the truck buyer with a much larger rear window that wrapped around the backside of the cab. It was a nice complement to the wraparound windshield found on the front of the cab. In order to provide for this option Ford had to really modify the rear cab panel to get the window to fit. The addition of this window option in combination with a "Custom Cab" package made for one sweet looking truck. It was a truck that matched in good looks anything that Chevrolet had to offer.

This brings us to the end of our coverage of Ford's "Economy Trucks" of the 1953 to 1956 periods. Over the years the trucks that came out of this time and era became some of the most popular and collectible Ford trucks of any era — definitely worthy successors to the "Bonus Built" Fords of the previous era.

Tonka released this 1953-'56 style Ford tow truck pressed steel toy in 1957. It looks like it has been well played with.

Typical Ford 1956 Custom Cab interior treatment. Note two-toned upholstery and door trim panels.

This promotional prototype shot shows the redesigned front grille and trim used on 1957 Ford F Series trucks. *Don Bunn Collection*

Chapter 7: Squared Off Looks and Tilting Cabs Too 1957-1960

The year 1957 was a year of big changes for the Ford Motor Company. All their cars and trucks were restyled to make them look more contemporary — especially the restyled looks of Ford's trucks. This new look was the first total redesign of their F Series trucks since they made their debut in 1948. This wasn't the only major news coming out of Dearborn this year. Along with these restyled regular Ford trucks the Ford people introduced a new car/truck hybrid they called the Ranchero. And then, to put the icing on the cake, Ford came out with a totally redesigned and engineered line of C Series trucks they called their Tilt Cabs.

New 1957 Ford F Series trucks featured slab-sided styling cues, which were in marked contrast to the rounded looks of previous Fords. The front fenders no longer bulged out as they did before. Now they were in line with the cab doors to provide for a flatter, more homogenous look. Ford added a bulge to the fender stamping around the wheel well to break up a too flat look and to highlight this area. They also added a character line that ran from the headlight pods through the doors and to the back of the cab to further reduce the too flat-sided look. The hoods on these trucks were quite a bit different as well. They were wider and flatter and no longer tapered down towards the front. Now they stretched all the way across the truck to completely cover the front fenders.

Once again Ford concentrated their efforts on these new trucks to develop a cab that would be more comfortable for the driver and passengers. These new cabs were wider and longer than the cabs used on the 1953 to 1956 models, which once again provided for more legroom, more hip room, and more shoulder room. Even the running boards were changed. No longer were they outside the cab. Ford relocated them inside the doors, which added to the more modern looks of these trucks. Other changes in these cabs could be seen in the dashboard, seats, and door panels, which took on a more upscale look. These cabs still used a wraparound windshield and regular and big back window options.

Ford's Medium-Duty F Series trucks were still the F-500 and F-600. The former was available in two wheelbase lengths, 130 and 154 inches. The F-600 was available in 130-, 142-, 154-, 172-, and 192-inch wheelbases.

Once again these trucks were available in Standard and Custom Cab forms. The latter included such niceties as dual sun visors, a perforated acoustic headliner covering a ½-inch-thick glass wool combination insulating pad, a dome light with manual switch, color-keyed three-toned upholstery fabrics, foam rubber padding in the seats, custom interior trim pieces, armrest on the driver's door, chrome-plated grille and headlight

This 1958 Ford F-500 Platform Body truck has found a home working on a ranch in Colorado.

This 1959 Ford F-600 butane truck has been dressed up a bit with a two-tone paint job, chrome-plated grille, bumper, and wheels.

FORD

'59 SCHOOL BUS CHASSIS B-500 · B-600 · B-700 · B-750

SCHOOL BUS

FORD

GO FORD-WARD FOR SAFETY AND SAVINGS!

Ford's truck selling theme for 1959 was to "Go Ford-Ward" as you can see on the front cover of this 1959 Ford catalog.

Here we see a 1959 Ford F-500 or F-600 truck in this promotional photograph that has been fitted with a frame-mounted crane setup.

pods, matched locks on doors, "Custom Cab" door plaques, bright metal rings around the parking lights, bright metal windshield band, sound deadener on floor and rear cab panels, fiberglass dashboard insulation, and attractive hardboard door and kick panels.

Though these changes to their F Series trucks were monumental Ford had even bigger changes in store for their C Series of trucks. Like their F Series counterparts these new C Series trucks looked entirely different from the Cab Forward COE trucks they replaced. Instead of just calling them their C Series of trucks Ford started referring to them as their "Tilt Cabs" because the major feature of these trucks was that the whole cab tilted forward allowing both major and minor maintenance work to be done with ease. With the cab tilted forward the mechanic could reach all over the engine or transmission without much effort.

These new cabs were a lot wider and had larger door openings than the old Cab Forward type of C Series truck. The glass areas in these cabs were also bigger than what came before making it easier for the driver to see all around the cab. A flat front end also allowed the driver to see more of what was in front of his truck making it easier to maneuver in the tight confines of city driving.

Another positive feature of this truck was its shorter front-to-rear-of-cab dimensions, which allowed the truck to carry a longer body or pull a longer trailer. In either case this extra room allowed the truck operator to carry larger payloads, which cut costs and improved profits. Another aspect of these trucks that also translated into greater load capacity was the fact that they employed set back front axles, which allowed more weight distribution between axles. That set back front axle when combined with this truck's wider tread also allowed the truck to be more stable. An added bonus of this combination was that these new C Series trucks had a shorter turning radius so one could drive and turn around on wide streets and thoroughfares without having to back up to complete a U-turn.

These Tilt Cab Fords also came with a new option that was the first to be used in a medium-duty or heavy-duty Ford truck — an automatic transmission. Ford offered an automatic transmission as an option in their light-duty trucks years before but this was the first time such a transmission would be offered in a large Ford truck. Ford called this transmission a Transmatic. The Transmatic had six forward speeds and was supplied to Ford by Allison Transmissions. The Transmatic made life a lot easier because drivers didn't have to constantly shift the truck between gears and, of course, didn't have to use a clutch.

Not all Ford trucks were redesigned for the 1957 model year. Case in point was Ford's P Series Parcel Delivery trucks. These trucks still used the front-end sheet metal that they did during the 1953 to 1956 era, and the grille that they used was the one that Ford had used for their 1955 models.

For 1958 all Ford trucks except the P Series featured dual headlights. Ford's F Series trucks also received a new grille treatment and redesigned exterior trim pieces. This new grille had a checkerboard type design instead of the single bar that was used in 1957.

The 223 cubic inch "Cost Clipper Six," which was now rated at 139 horsepower, was still the standard engine found in most light-duty and medium-duty rated Ford trucks this year. However, if you were a medium-duty Ford truck buyer and wanted a V-8 sitting under the hood there were two engine choices available to you. Both of them displaced 292 cubic inches and one was rated as a regular-duty power plant while the other was referred to as a 292 HD — the "HD" stood for heavy-duty. The regular 292 had a horsepower rating of 186 while the 292 HD bettered that mark by 1 horsepower, which brought it up to 187.

For 1959 the Ford truck lineup now consisted of 370 different models in the F, B, C, T, P, and

A 1960 Ford F-600 Custom Cab equipped dump truck is shown in this promotional photograph. Judging by the fact that it is wearing a silver-painted grille, this truck was probably a prototype. *Ford Motor Company Photograph*

Ford's restyled "gear and lightning bolt" emblem that appeared on some Ford trucks in 1960. This one has never been used on a truck and is still in its original box.

A tree trimming company in New Mexico uses this 1959 Ford F-600 truck to haul away yard wastes.

Ranchero Series. The F, B, and some T Series truck models received a redesigned hood this year. This hood had a vent panel located on its front side. In the middle of that vent Ford put a set of large F O R D letters. Along with this new hood design one could also see that the grille and the parking light design had been changed as well. This new grille for the 1959 Fords consisted of a series of horizontal bars that connected the headlight pods. The parking lamp design change could be seen on light-duty and medium-duty F Series trucks. The new design was done in a rectangular shape rather than in a circular shape as was seen on the 1958 models.

Ford's Custom Cab models looked even fancier this year in both their new interior and exterior treatments. Inside a new white steering wheel was used, while the Standard model Fords still used a black steering wheel. The white steering wheel came with a chrome-plated horn ring, an item missing on Standard models. The door

panels and the dashboards were painted in a two-tone finish that made these trucks look that much fancier. Chrome plating was used to trim out the gauge cluster and was also used around the parking lamps below the restyled chrome-plated grille.

Custom Cab seat upholstery was done up in a woven vinyl candy motif and once again these covers were placed over thick foam rubber padding. Other upgrades seen in the interior were dual sun visors and an illuminated cigar lighter. Features in this package included extra insulating pads to quiet the cabs, a fancy looking headliner, and a metal band around the windshield. These trucks looked especially nice when ordered with a two-tone paint job. In that instance white paint was used on the hood and upper door areas while a complementary solid color was used on the roof panel and below the character line.

The year 1960 was another year of improvements for these new Fords. Ford fitted them with improved brakes, clutches, heavier-duty springs, and better cooling systems. Ford also made some improvements to their truck engines to make them perform better and at the same time provide better fuel economy ratings.

The number of Ford truck models available this year jumped again and now stood at just under 500.

Ford's F, B, and some T models were treated to a new grille again this year. Their hoods were also redesigned and instead of one large vent in the front like we saw in 1959 the 1960 hood had two vent slots that were separated by a restyled Ford truck crest emblem.

The F-500, F-600, C-550, and C-600 models were treated to newer, sturdier frames this year and the F-600 truck buyer could order an optional double channel heavy-duty frame to go along with heavier-duty front and rear axles and springs for a higher GVW rating. When ordered in such a fashion a truck buyer could get a heavy-duty rated truck for the price of a medium-duty unit.

Here is another 1959 Ford F-600 flatbed truck that was spotted at a truck show in California.

As we said in the beginning of this chapter these Ford trucks looked entirely different than the trucks they replaced. Some people prefer the looks of the earlier trucks because of their "classic" 1950s styling cues. If you want to stand out from the crowd you might consider picking up one of these "slab-sided" Fords. As far as trucks go they are just as good as earlier models and if you like your trucks loaded these trucks were offered with more optional equipment.

This 1960 Ford tanker truck is spraying water on a field to keep the dust down during a truck show.

Painted in an orange color this 1961 Ford dump truck looks like an ex-highway department truck.

Chapter 8: A New Look and More New Models from Which to Choose 1961-1966

Ford started off the 1960s decade with redesigned F, B, and T Series trucks along with a new line of small economy trucks and a line hauler semi tractor-trailer type truck. The former was called the Econoline while Ford referred to the latter as their H Series. The Econoline was a series of unibody trucks that were available as pickups, vans, or station buses. The H Series trucks used a modified Tilt Cab body that was mounted high on the frame. The H Series was also the first Ford truck that was offered for sale here in the USA

with a Cummins V-8 diesel engine. Or if a gasoline engine was more to your liking the H Series trucks were available with Ford Super-Duty V-8s. The Econoline was an economy truck that was available with a small, economical Ford 6-cylinder engine like that used in the Falcon.

Ford's medium-duty F Series trucks, like their light and heavy-duty versions, featured new cabs in combination with restyled front-end treatments. This restyling job did away with the slab-sided look that was prevalent on these trucks during the 1957 to 1960 period. The cabs themselves were roomier on the inside while on the outside they featured more body sculpturing, rounded curves and corners, wider and flatter hoods, and a larger windshield and back cab window. The front fender panels on the medium and heavy-duty F Series trucks were bowed out a bit this year, so as to provide some extra clearance for the wider axles and larger tires that were installed on these trucks.

Up front a new grille design and single headlights replaced the dual headlights that had appeared on these trucks since the 1958 model year. The grille treatment was a much simpler affair than what was used on the previous trucks. A set of two parallel bars that connected to the headlight pods was the grille motif chosen for the light and medium-duty F Series trucks while the heavier-duty units featured a totally different look that consisted of two extruded metal sections separated by a center section of smaller horizontal bars that covered the radiator. The word F O R D was spelled out in letters that were located between the two bars used in the light and medium-duty trucks along with their parking lamps. On the heavier-duty trucks the F O R D letters appeared on the upper portion of the grille surround panel.

Ford's medium-duty trucks this year came equipped with stronger frames, springs, brakes, etc. Wheelbases available on these trucks included 132-, 144-, 156-, 174-, and 194-inch lengths. Before the 1961 model year Ford's Medium-Duty F Series line of trucks was made up of F-500 and F-600 models but this year Ford expanded this line to include F-700 models. These trucks came with stronger frames and heavier-duty springs and axles. They were also available with either 292 or 302 cubic inch heavy-duty V-8 engines.

Engines for the 1961 Ford F-500 Series included the 223 cubic inch overhead valve 6-cylinder or a 292 cubic inch V-8 as an extra cost option. The F-600 also came standard with the 223 cubic inch 6-cylinder engine and two 292 cubic inch

This colorful magazine ad from 1961 promotes Ford's new "Big Six" engine option.

V-8s as options. However, if a buyer wanted to pay a little extra for a bigger 6-cylinder engine for his F-600, Ford had one available. Ford called this engine their "Big Six" and it was heavily promoted in their advertising campaigns of 1961. Basically this 262 cubic inch "Big Six" was a bored and stroked version of the smaller 223 cubic inch engine. It carried a horsepower rating of 152 and, though it was an extra cost option for the F-600, Ford offered it as the standard engine in the C-550 and C-600 Tilt Cab trucks this year.

For 1962 Ford's F-100 through F-600 models featured another grille design change to help

Somebody converted this 1961 Ford School Bus into a camper and it looks like it could use a little tender loving care.

distinguish them from the 1961 models. This grille design still used two parallel bars but instead of these bars being separated by the F O R D letters a stylized star design was placed in the area between these two bars. The Ford name was spelled out in smaller block letters in a panel just above the grille opening. The F-700 and F-750 trucks still used the 1961 style grille and Ford's B Series School Bus Chassis also used the 1961 type grille.

Ford also added another series of trucks to their Medium-Duty Line this year and those trucks were their F-750 models. These trucks were actually downgraded heavy-duty models. We look on them as medium-duty trucks because they used medium-duty F-700 frames and medium-duty front fenders and trim. Under their hoods though these trucks were powered by bigger more powerful heavy-duty V-8 engines that displaced 332 cubic inches. By the combination of medium-duty and heavy-duty parts one could call these trucks medium-heavies.

Ford's truck line for the 1963 model year had grown to cover more than 1,000 models. The Ford Truck Division also took this opportunity to introduce a new series of trucks to the market — a series they called their N Series. The new N Series of trucks were basically short nose versions of Ford's F Series. They used the same cab, frames,

springs, axles, engines, transmissions, and other assorted pieces from the F Series. The parts that were different were the hoods, grilles, and front fenders. Actually the grille and front end treatment used on these N Series Ford trucks was a modified version of the front end equipment used on the heavy-duty F Series and H Series of Ford trucks.

This new N Series of trucks offered the best of both worlds between a Tilt Cab truck and a conventional one. It offered a shorter bumper-

This 1963 Ford F-500 with a Gerstenslager Body was used as an ambulance and rescue unit for the McCook, Nebraska, area. It was then converted into a salvage unit when its days as a rescue unit were over. *Dennis J. Maag*

to-back-of-cab dimension like a tilt cab with the comfort and conveniences found in a regular truck cab. That shorter front-bumper-to-back-of-cab length allowed this truck to carry a longer body or pull a longer trailer for increased payloads. The shorter nose on these trucks allowed the driver to see everything in front of the cab better as well as making it easier for the driver to maneuver these trucks especially in the tight confines of cities and towns. Ford at that time was charging higher prices for their Tilt Cabs than for their conventional cab trucks. A truck buyer could save some money by buying an N Series truck with all the good points attributed to a Tilt Cab Ford without having to pay the higher price for one.

Also new to the Ford truck lineup this year was the addition of diesel engines in medium and heavy-duty ranks. One of these engines, offered as an option in the C and N Series of Ford trucks, was a 330 cubic inch 6-cylinder engine that had a horsepower rating of 112. The second diesel engine was a smaller 4-cylinder unit that Ford offered as an option in their P Series Panel Delivery truck chassis. This engine displaced 220 cubic inches and carried a horsepower rating of 70. Both engines were designed and manufactured by Ford of England and saw millions of miles of dependable service in European Ford trucks.

Ford Diesel Engine Specifications

	Ford 220	Ford 330
Number of Cylinders	4, In-Line	6, In-Line
Bore and Stroke	3.94 x 4.52 inches	3.94 x 4.52 inches
Cubic Inch Displacement	220	330
Maximum Gross Horsepower	70 at 2,500 rpm	112 at 2,500 rpm
Maximum Net Horsepower	65 at 2,500 rpm	104 at 2,500 rpm
Maximum Gross Torque	160 at 1,600 rpm	265 at 1,500 rpm
Maximum Net Torque	156 ft/lbs at 1,550 rpm	262 ft/lbs at 1,500 rpm
Compression Ratio	16 to 1	16 to 1
Cylinder Block and Head	Alloy Cast Iron	Alloy Cast Iron
Camshaft	5 bearing, Special Cast Iron	7 bearing, Special Cast Iron
Crankshaft	Counter Balanced Steel Forged	Counter Balance Steel Forged
Main Bearings	Copper- Lead Replaceable Insert	Copper-Lead Replaceable Insert
Connecting Rods	Forged Steel I-Beam	Forged Steel I-Beam
Pistons	Aluminum Alloy	Aluminum Alloy
Piston Pins	Full Floating Steel	Full Floating Steel
Valves	Poppet Type	Poppet Type
Push Rods	Tubular Steel	Tubular Steel
Rocker Arms	Adjustable Forged Steel	Adjustable Forged Steel
Firing Order	1-2-4-3	1-5-3-6-2-4
Electrical System	12 Volt	12 Volt
Oil System Capacity	8 3/4	12
Normal Oil Pressure (Hot)	35 psi at 1,500 rpm	35 psi at 1,500 rpm

When it comes to N Series Ford trucks it is hard to tell the 1963-1965 trucks apart because they all look pretty much the same.

Want to change your medium-duty Ford truck into a heavy-duty model. Just extend the frame and add a tandem rear axle setup just like they did to this 1964 Ford F-600.

This truck with a utility body mounted on its frame looks to be a 1965 Ford F-600 model.

According to the vehicle history card taped on the windshield of this C-600 Tilt Cab truck it is a 1966 model that was built by Ford's Holman & Moody Racing Team to haul their race cars across the country.

The big news coming from the Ford truck world in 1964 was the news that Ford was introducing a new family of Ford gasoline truck engines for their medium and heavy-duty trucks. Ford termed this new series their "FT" engines. "FT" translated to Ford Truck. These new engines, all V-8s, were available in 330 cubic inches, 361 cubic inches, and 391 cubic inches. These engines were basically truck versions of Ford's "FE" Series of car engines. Most of these new Ford "FT" engines contained forged crankshafts, rotating valves, double timing chains, and heavy-duty connecting rods. These engines were optional for F-600 and higher heavier-duty trucks.

Another change seen in the F-500 Series of trucks this year was their use of heavier-duty frames, which were formerly used under the F-600. Along with the heavier-duty frames for these trucks came heavier-duty axles, springs, and shock absorbers. The F-600 frames were beefed up this year as well. The F-700 and F-750 trucks also received stronger frames, springs, and axles, which gave them higher GVW ratings. These higher GVW ratings moved them once again back into Ford's heavy-duty ranks.

Moving ahead to the 1965 model year the big news once again concerned new engines for Ford trucks. This time around these new engines

This beautiful two-tone painted Ford N-700 Custom Cab truck with its high stake body was used for years to haul boxes of strawberries from the farm to markets in cities and towns.

were not V-8s but instead were 6-cylinder types. The smaller of the two new 6-cylinder engines released this year was a 240 cubic inch unit that was rated at 150 horsepower at 4,000 rpm. The second new 6-cylinder engine was Ford's new 300 cubic inch unit, which had a maximum horsepower rating of 170 at 3,600 rpm. The horsepower was pretty good for these engines but their torque ratings were higher at lower RPMs. The 240 had a maximum torque rating of 234 ft/lbs at 2,200 rpm while the 300 had a maximum torque rating of 283 ft/lbs between 1,400 and 2,400 rpm. That was a high torque rating for an engine of this size over such a wide RPM band. The 240 was the standard engine for most Ford trucks up to and including the F-500, while the

300 was the standard engine for the F-600. There was also a heavy-duty version of the 300 available for those who wanted a tougher engine. All these engines, which replaced the 223 and the 262 "Big Six" featured thin wall casting techniques, 4-inch bores, hydraulic valve lifters, crankshafts supported by seven main bearings, stud-mounted rocker arms, and cams driven by gears. When all was said and done these new Ford 6-cylinder engines were lighter, more powerful, and more economical than the engines they replaced.

For Ford light-duty truck fans this was the year that Ford introduced their famous "Twin I-Beam" front axles. And, of course, Ford's light-duty and medium-duty trucks were freshened up a bit with a restyled grille. This time around the grille treatment

This "low top" Ford N Series truck was spotted at a swap meet. The guy who owned it used it to haul all of his vintage sheet metal to the swap meet in hopes of selling everything.

1965 Ford Truck Engine Choices For Medium-Duty Vehicles

240 cubic inch 6	150 hp at 4,000 rpm	234 ft/lbs of Torque at 2,200 rpm
300 cubic inch 6	170 hp at 3,600 rpm	283 ft/lbs of Torque at 1,400-2,400 rpm
300 cubic inch 6 HD	170 hp at 3,600 rpm	283 ft/lbs of Torque at 1,400-2,400 rpm
330 cubic inch V-8	186 hp at 4,000 rpm	300 ft/lbs of Torque at 2,000 rpm
330 cubic inch HD V-8	186 hp at 4,000 rpm	300 ft/lbs of Torque at 2,000 rpm

included a design that used a series of vertical lines in combination with some horizontal lines.

The only major news involving Ford trucks for the 1966 model year was the introduction of Ford's new Bronco Utility Vehicle to their light-duty lineup and a new major roof redesign for Ford F-Series (F-800 and above), T, and N Series of trucks. This new redesign had Ford raising the roofs of these trucks through the use of a modified roof panel. This raised roof change allowed the drivers and passengers to have more headroom than the unmodified cab versions. Also of major news later on in the model year was the announcement that Ford was replacing their H Series of trucks with a new series. This new series was called the "W Series" and it looked totally different than the H Series of trucks it replaced.

Over the course of this six-year period Ford introduced a number of new models, new engines, both gasoline and diesel fueled, and handsomely restyled trucks to the marketplace. Truck buyers responded in a positive manner to all of these changes and new additions by buying even more of these new Fords than the trucks Ford offered back in the 1950s. This pleasant state of affairs increased Ford's market share in total sales, which is the primary reason Ford made all the changes they did during this time. If you are a collector of Ford trucks you will find a lot to choose from when selecting a Ford from these years.

1967 Ford F-600 Custom Cab truck shown at a construction site. *Ford Motor Company Photograph*

Chapter 9: A New Look for the F Series and New Trucks From Louisville 1967-1972

For the first time since the 1961 model year Ford's F Series trucks went through a major restyling job. The only trucks whose looks didn't change were Ford's heavy-duty and extra heavy-duty trucks higher than the F-750. These trucks still retained the 1961 to 1966 style cabs (raised roofs), hoods, front fenders, grilles, bumpers, and other associated parts. All the other F Series Ford trucks from the F-100 through the F-750 got new restyled cabs that were roomier and more comfort-

able than the previously used cabs for these trucks. Inside these new cabs contained more headroom, more legroom, and more shoulder and hip room. The seats were wider now and mounted higher off the floor. In the medium-duty and higher rated trucks a new 20-inch-diameter steering wheel allowed the driver to steer these trucks with less effort. The steering column that these steering wheels were mounted on was placed in a more upright position so the driver found it easier to get by the steering column with less effort. These trucks had redesigned instrument panels and higher quality materials covering the seats.

The exterior styling of these redesigned cabs featured wider, flatter hoods, an extruded character bulge line that ran from the front of the truck to the back on pickups and other light-duty models. This character line on heavier-duty trucks ran through the doors and the back of the cab tying these components to the front fenders. Those front fenders on the medium and heavy-duty trucks were taller and had wheel wells that were larger to accommodate taller tires and the wider front axles used on these trucks. Those fenders framed a much taller, wider, and heavier looking grille as well. On standard models that grille was painted white while the Custom Cab deluxe models used a grille with a bright metal finish. By combining all these elements, the wider grille, larger and wider fenders, wider cabs, and flatter hoods, these trucks now looked bigger and presented a more massive appearance. Even the medium-duty Ford trucks now looked like their bigger, heavier-duty rated counterparts.

As we stated earlier these new Ford trucks used an eight inch wider front axle which helped to reduce turning diameters and made these trucks easier to operate especially in tight situations.

Once again Ford's Medium-Duty Truck Line this year included the F-500, F-600, N-500, C-550, C-600, N-600, B-500, B-600, and some P Series trucks. Diesel engines were offered as options in all 600-rated trucks. When equipped with a diesel engine the 600 designation became 6000.

Standard engine in the 500 Series trucks this year was Ford's 240 cubic inch 6-cylinder while the base engine in the 600 trucks was once again the 300 cubic inch heavy-duty six. Optional engines for the F-500 were the 300 cubic inch six and a 330 cubic inch V-8. Optional engines for trucks in Ford's 600 ratings were the 330 cubic inch V-8, 330 cubic inch Heavy-Duty V-8, 361

A retired 1967 Ford C Series Tilt Cab trucks put out to pasture in Colorado circa 1998.

The last time we were in Winslow, Arizona, we looked for a girl in a Ford truck but all we could find was this 1967 Ford F-600 tow truck.

cubic inch Heavy-Duty V-8, and a 363 cubic inch 6-cylinder diesel engine.

No matter which engine was chosen Ford made sure that these engines were easy to work on especially in their F Series of trucks. These new F Series trucks featured extra wide engine compartments making it easier to reach and service most components.

A 1967 Ford F-700 tractor-trailer gets ready to pull a trailer away from a loading dock in Kansas City, Missouri, in 2003.

Dashboard layout on a late 1960s Ford F Series truck.

F-500 truck buyers had three wheelbase choices this year with lengths available in 132, 156, and 174 inches, while F-600 buyers could choose from wheelbases of 132, 156, 174, and 194 inches. F-600 trucks with 194-inch wheelbases came with heavier-duty frames as well.

Standard cab equipped Ford medium-duty trucks this year came with a beige colored vinyl seat cover, padded sun visors, a padded dash cover, a glove box, a dome light, a molded fiberglass headliner, and a fresh air heater at no extra charge. Custom Cab versions came with a white steering wheel, a bright metal finished grille, "Custom Cab" badges, a bright metal finished windshield band, deep foam padding in the seat, a cigarette lighter, red, green, blue, or beige woven plastic seat cover color-coordinated to the exterior cab color, extra insulation in different cab areas, and a custom fitted perforated hardboard headliner. Both cabs were over 65 inches wide at their widest point allowing three full size men to fit in the cab comfortably. As an added bonus truck buyers could now order integral air conditioning in these cabs as an extra cost option.

Though they didn't look much different than the 1967 models they replaced Ford did make some improvements to their 1968 model trucks. On their exteriors the medium-duty Fords got reflectors added to their hood side trim and side marker lights mounted on their front fenders.

For truck buyers who needed to transport a crew to the job site Ford added a new cab option to the F-600 lineup this year. This new cab option was a four-door "Crew Cab" that was available on all 2-wheel-drive F-600 trucks under a Domestic Special Order program.

Once again Ford offered F-600 buyers the option of ordering their trucks powered by a 6-cylinder diesel engine instead of a gasoline engine. In addition to that engine option Ford offered their F-600 and C-600 buyers another more powerful diesel engine option. Ford called these engines their "V Series Diesel Engines" and when one of these was ordered in an F Series truck it became an F-6000. The same could be said for the C-600. With one of these engines under its cab it became a C-6000. Caterpillar built these engines for Ford and they were called the "V-150" and the "V-175." Both engines were V-8s and both displaced 522 cubic inches. The "V-150" carried a maximum horsepower rating of 150 while the "V-175" had a maximum rating of 175 horsepower. Maximum torque ratings for the "V-150" were 302 ft/lbs at 1,800 rpm and the "V-175" carried a maximum torque rating of 352 ft/lbs at 1,800 rpm.

1968 Ford F-500 Standard Equipment Specification Sheet

Engine: Ford 240 cubic inch 6-Cylinder
Alternator: Autolite 42 amp/hr 630 Watt
Front Axle: Ford 5000 LB Rated
Rear Axle: Rockwell C-100 11,000 LB Rated
Rear Axle Ratio: 6.2:1
Battery: 12 Volt 55 amp/hr
Service Brakes: Self Adjusting Front: 14 x 2½ inch Drum, Rear: 15 x 4 inch Drum
Vacuum Booster
Parking Brake: Bendix Internal Shoe 9 x 2-inch mounted on rear of transmission
Clutch: Heavy-Duty 11-inch size
Frame: Single Channel Steel, 36,000 psi rating
Fuel Tank: 19.5 Gallons, In-cab mount
Front Springs: Leaf Type, 1,750 LB capacity
Rear Springs: Radius Leaf Type, 4,500 LB capacity
Steering Box: Gemmer 375
Transmission: New Process 425 Synchronized 4-Speed Direct Manual
Tires: Front and Dual Rear 7.00 x 20-inch, 8-Ply Rating
Wheels: 6 Hole Disc (6) 20 x 5-inch Rim Size

A close up view of a Ford 600 side badge as used on N Series trucks back in the 1960s.

Amoco used this 1968 Ford F-600 fire truck at their Wood River, Illinois, complex until it was closed in the mid 1990s.
Dennis J. Maag

1968 Ford F-500 Standard Equipment

Dual Armrests
Ammeter and Oil Pressure Gauges
Speedometer
Backup Lights
Front Channel Bumper
DeLuxe Heater and Defroster
Single Electronic Horn
5 I.C.C. Cab Clearance Lights
I.C.C. Transistorized Emergency Flasher
2 Marker Lights Mounted on Front Fenders
Left-Hand Exterior Mirror
Padded Dash Pad
Padded Sun Visors
Running Boards
Seat Belts
Double Faced Fender-Mounted Front Turn Signal Lamps
Rear Taillights
Windshield Washers
Two-Speed Electric Windshield Wipers

Here we see a nice looking 1968 C-750 Tilt Cab tractor displayed at a California truck show.

Ford's N Series trucks were in production from 1963 through 1969, when they were replaced by Ford's L Series trucks.

Optional Rear Axles and Ratios:

Rockwell C-100	11,000 LB rating	6.8:1 ratio	Single Speed
Rockwell D-100	13,000 LB rating	5.83:1, 6.2:1, 6.8:1 ratios	Single Speed
Rockwell F-106	15,000 LB rating	6.2:1, 6.8:1, 7.2:1 ratios	Single Speed
Eaton 13802	15,000 LB rating	5.83:1/8.12:1 or 6.33:1/8.81:1	Two Speed

1968 F-600 Standard Equipment Specification Sheet

Engine: Ford 300 cubic inch Heavy-Duty 6-Cylinder Gasoline Fueled

Alternator: Autolite 42 amp/hr 630 Watt

Front Axle: Ford 5,000 LB rating

Rear Axle: Rockwell F-106 15,000 LB rating 6.2:1 ratio

Battery: 12 Volt 55 amp/hr

Service Brakes: Self Adjusting Vacuum/Hydraulic Front: 14 x 2½-inch Drum, Rear: 15 x 4-inch Drum

Parking Brake: Bendix Internal Shoe 9 x 2-inch mounted on back of transmission

Clutch: 12 inch

Frame: Single Channel 36,000 psi rating Section Modulus: 132-174 inch wb 9.45 inch high, Section Modulus: 194 inch wb 11.84 inch high

Fuel Tank: 19.5 Gallons In-Cab Mounted Tank

Front Springs: 2,600 LB rating

Rear Springs: 6,700 LB rating

Steering Box: Gemmer 375

Transmission: New Process 4-Speed Synchronized Direct Manual

Tires: Tube Type 7.50 x 20-inch 8-Ply rating

Wheels: (6) Six Hole Disc 20 x 6-inch size

1968 Ford F-600 Standard Equipment List

Dual Armrests

Ammeter and Oil pressure Gauges

Speedometer

Backup Lights

Front Bumper

DeLuxe Fresh Air Heater and Defroster

Single Electric Horn

5 I.C.C. Cab Clearance Lights

I.C.C. Emergency Lamp Flasher Transistorized System

2 Front Fender Marker Lights
Left-Hand Mirror
Padded Dashboard Cover
Padded Sun Visors
Running Boards
Seat Belts
Double Faced Front Fender-Mounted Turn Signals
Rear Taillights
Two Speed Windshield Wipers
Windshield Washers

The owner of this 1969 Ford C Series flatbed truck has dressed it up with double chrome-plated front bumpers, dual exhaust stacks, and an American flag.

Ford finished off the 1968 model year by scoring the top position in truck sales and for 1969 they wanted to accomplish the same feat. To reach that goal Ford offered over 800 different truck models and they opened up a number of Ford Truck Centers throughout the country. The purpose of these specialized truck centers was to sell, service, and stock parts for Ford's Medium, Heavy, and Extra Heavy-Duty trucks.

Ford made some changes to their trucks in spring and axles options, transmission options, and some minor changes in trim and appearance items. Ford also started to use a new industry wide standard on rating their frames for their medium-duty and higher rated trucks.

During this year Ford also started supplying some of their P Series Parcel Delivery Chassis to the motor home manufacturing industry for conversion purposes. Ford started installing some of their 363 cubic inch 6-cylinder diesel engines in P-500 Parcel Delivery Chassis models. When such a combination was ordered Ford referred to these models as P-5000 units.

At the end of the model year Ford had done it again, finishing first in the truck sales race by selling even more trucks than they had the previous year. The total for the 1968 model year was over 713,700 units sold and in 1969 Ford beat that mark by over

This promotional photograph was released by the Ford Motor Company in the Summer of 1971 to promote the new 1972 C Series and F Series trucks. *Ford Motor Company Photograph*

32,100 units with sales over 745,800 units.

The big news for Ford trucks for the 1970 model year was the opening in the summer of 1969 of Ford's new and massive heavy truck plant in Louisville, Kentucky. This new plant Ford called their Kentucky Truck Plant. Besides celebrating the opening of this new plant Ford took the opportunity in the fall of 1969 of introducing a new line of trucks. In honor of where these new trucks were built Ford referred to this new series as their "Louisville Line," or L Series, for short.

These new L Series trucks featured all new cabs and a fiberglass front-end clip that integrated the hood, front fenders, and grille into a single cohesive unit. This integrated lightweight fiberglass unit, that was supported by a steel frame, could be tilted forward to provide access to the engine, transmission, brakes, and other assorted systems and components for easy maintenance work. If a truck buyer needed a regular hood on a truck and a non-tilting front end he could also order one of these trucks with a 'butterfly' style two-piece opening hood. In that case the front fenders, hood, and grille piece were all separate units.

These new Ford trucks featured large, roomy, comfortable cab interiors along with increased glass areas in the windshield, doors, and back of the cab. These interiors were also fitted with high quality materials and they were designed to minimize noise and vibrations being transmitted into the cab. Ford designers also designed these cabs to provide just the right amount of floor-to-roof room, and side-to-side room, to provide a comfortable environment for drivers and passengers alike.

Underneath these new cabs Ford chose to use new premium steel frames that were stronger than some multiple channel frames used by competitors. By using such high tensile strength steel in these frames Ford could make them lighter than the competition. With weight-saving devices like this these trucks would be more economical to run.

Though these trucks used conventional cabs their wide track front axles allowed them to maneuver as well as some "snub-nose" or other shorter cab models. Their short back of cab to front bumpers also allowed truck buyers to install longer bodies on their frames. Ford also offered them with different length wheelbases to which different length bodies could be mounted. For medium-duty truck buyers the LN-500 and LN-600 were the Medium-Duty rated trucks of this new "Louisville Line."

Like other Ford trucks in 1970 these new L Series trucks were available in Standard or Custom Cab trim levels. The Standard model cab included the following equipment: a hardboard headlining, padded instrument panel, padded sun visors, heavy-duty rubber floor mat, fresh air heater/defroster, all weather ventilation, bench or individual seats, cab back trim panel with diesels and individual seats, cab back insulation for trucks with diesel engines, a glove compartment, seat belts, dome light, double yoke door locks, coat hook, 6 x 16-inch Western Style mirrors, 5 I.C.C. clearance lights, fender-mounted turn signal lamps, electric horn, combination stop, turn signal, and rear lamps, exterior cab assist handle on left side, reversible ignition and door key, and side reflectors on front fenders. In addition to that equipment the Custom Cab models offered padded vinyl door trim panels, cigarette lighter, armrests on both doors, deluxe varitone floor mat, cab back trim and insulation panel, left door courtesy dome light switch, basket weave patterned vinyl trim on bench seats, breathable knitted vinyl coverings on individual seats, bright anodized aluminum grille, a bright metal windshield band, a bright plated cab assist handle on the right side, pedestal-mounted roof clearance lights, and roof panel insulation.

Ford's L Series cabs also featured a deep dip "electrocoated" prime painting process. This process had Ford dipping these cabs into a large vat of primer paint that is electrically charged so that besides coating the easy to reach pieces the primer is drawn into and coats the inaccessible areas to help ward off corrosion. This special painting system also provided a better bonding process for the coats of paint that were applied over the primer coat. As an added protection against future rust problems the bottom areas of these cabs were zinc coated before the primer was applied. All that protection might be the main reason why we see so many of these early L Series trucks still on the road today.

These new Ford L Series trucks also came equipped with the same engines, transmissions, and other components that were available on other Ford trucks this year like the F, C, B, and W Series models.

Besides Ford's "Louisville Line" the Kentucky Truck Plant complex built Ford's C Tilt Cab trucks, Ford's Heavy-Duty F Series trucks, and W Series trucks. Production of F-500, F-600, P Series Panel Deliveries, and B Series School Bus vehicles were built in other plants this year.

With the introduction of Ford's "Louisville Line" of medium, heavy, and extra heavy-duty trucks in 1970, Ford didn't need their N Series trucks anymore so they were dropped at the end of the 1969 model year. The same can be said for the Extra Heavy-Duty F Series trucks that were a mainstay in the Ford truck lineup since 1961.

For truck buyers who had a need to take their trucks off-road at times in 1971 Ford offered a factory built 4x4 version of their F-600 trucks. Prior to 1971 if buyers wanted a 4x4 vehicle in a medium-duty or higher rated truck they had to go to an outside conversion firm like Marmon-Herrington for such a vehicle. Now buyers could order one directly from their local Ford dealer.

These new Ford F-600 4x4 trucks were offered with 330 cubic inch V-8 gasoline engines as standard equipment. That engine was combined with a Warner-Gear T-19 4-speed synchronized manual transmission. They also came with a 2-speed transfer case and a heavy-duty Rockwell front axle.

Other new changes for Ford's F-600 trucks in 1971 were the company's offering of two new Cab and Chassis models. One came with a 180-inch wheelbase while the other came with a longer 212-inch wheelbase.

The model year of 1972 saw a number of changes for Ford's truck line. For the F-500 and B-500 trucks and buses the 240 cubic inch 6-cylinder engine was dropped and the 300 cubic inch 6-cylinder engine became the base powerplant for these vehicles.

For F-600 truck customers who wanted an automatic transmission in their trucks Ford offered a modified 3-speed Cruise-O-Matic transmission as an option this year. For buyers of other F, B, C, and LN trucks Ford offered an Allison built 4-speed automatic transmission in some models as well.

Another new Ford F-600 Chassis and Cab model was offered this year and this one used a 186-inch wheelbase. These Ford trucks were popular with farmers who liked them because they could accommodate longer aftermarket-sourced grain bodies.

Ford's Truck and Tractor Divisions cooperated on a joint project this year in producing a special F-600 truck that had a Ford backhoe built on the back of its chassis. This unit combined the best features of a medium-duty truck with the utility of a tractor. Not too many people knew about this truck project, which might explain why only a few of them were produced. The idea behind this combination was that a farmer or a contractor could drive this unit into a field or to a job site and set up to start digging a trench or a hole. By having a single unit they wouldn't have to tow a trailer with a tractor to the work area.

Ford also dropped some models from their truck lineups this year. Among them were the C-500, LN-500, P-600, B-6000, and the P-4000 models.

When all was said and done this was another successful period for Ford trucks. During this time Ford produced some great trucks, introduced some new models, and opened one of the world's largest and most efficient truck plants. All of these actions helped Ford to increase their market share even further during this period at a very competitive time for truck manufacturers.

Original Ford Truck Base Prices 1967-1972

1967

F-500 Chassis and Cab	$2985
F-500 Stake Body (132-inch wb)	$3245
F-500 Platform Body -(132-inch wb)	$3185
F-500 Stake Body (156-inch wb)	$3330
F-500 Stake Body (156-inch wb)	$3245
N-500 Chassis and Cab	$3245
N-500 Stake Body (121-inch wb)	$3500
N-500 Platform Body (121-inch wb)	$3430
N-500 Stake Body -(144-inch wb)	$3605
N-500 Platform Body -(144-inch wb)	$3510
C-550 Chassis with Tilt Cab	$3890
C-550 Stake Body -(111-inch wb)	$4210
C-550 -Platform Body (111-inch wb)	$4115
P-400 Panel Delivery Chassis	$2050
P-500 Parcel Delivery Chassis	$2270
P-4000 Parcel Delivery Chassis	$3215
P-5000 Parcel Delivery Chassis	$3450
B-500 School Bus Chassis	$2555
F-600 Chassis with Cab	$3300
F-600 Stake Body (132-inch wb)	$3570
F-600 Platform Body (132-inch wb)	$3500
F-600 Stake Body (156-inch wb)	$3650
F-600 Platform Body (156-inch wb)	$3560
N-600 Chassis with Cab	$3425
N-600 Stake Body (121-inch wb)	$3675
N-600 Platform Body (121-inch wb)	$3610
N-600 Stake Body (144-inch wb)	$3780
N-600 Platform Body (144-inch wb)	$3690
C-600 Chassis with Cab	$4230
C-600 Stake Body (111-inch wb)	$4520
C-600 Platform Body (111-inch wb)	$4460
B-600 School Bus Chassis	$2810
F-6000 Chassis and Cab	$5465
F-6000 Stake Body (132-inch wb)	$5740
F-6000 Platform Body (132-inch wb)	$5665
C-6000 Chassis with Tilt Cab	$6350
N-6000 Chassis with Cab	$5480
N-6000 Stake Body (121-inch wb)	$5750
N-6000 Platform Body (121-inch wb)	$5680
N-6000 Stake Body (144-inch wb)	$5865
N-6000 Platform Body (144-inch wb)	$5765
B-6000 School Bus Chassis	$5065

1968

F-500 Chassis and Cab	$3270
F-500 Stake Body (132-inch wb)	$3570
F-500 Platform Body (132-inch wb)	$3495
F-500 Stake Body (156-inch wb)	$3650
F-500 Platform Body (156-inch wb)	$3565
N-500 Chassis and Cab	$3500
N-500 Stake Body (121-inch wb)	$3800
N-500 Platform Body (121-inch wb)	$3730
N-500 Stake Body (144-inch wb)	$3900
N-500 Platform Body (144-inch wb)	$3810
C-550 Chassis with Tilt Cab	$4160
C-550 Stake Body (111-inch wb)	$4560
C-550 Platform Body (111-inch wb)	$4520
B-500 School Bus Chassis	$2880
C-600 Chassis with Tilt Cab	$4550
C-600 Stake Body (111-inch wb)	$4865
C-600 Platform Body (111-inch wb)	$4815
F-600 Chassis with Cab	$3560
F-600 Stake Body (132-inch wb)	$3865
F-600 Platform Body (132-inch wb)	$3800
F-600 Stake Body (156-inch wb)	$3950
F-600 Platform Body (156-inch wb)	$3855
N-600 Chassis with Cab	$3660
N-600 Stake Body (121-inch wb)	$3950
N-600 Platform Body (121-inch wb)	$3880
N-600 Stake Body (144-inch wb)	$4055
N-600 Platform Body (144-inch wb)	$3960
B-600 School Bus Chassis	$3160
P-400 Parcel Delivery Chassis	$2170
P-500 Parcel Delivery Chassis	$2385
P-4000 Parcel Delivery Chassis	$3310
P-5000 Parcel Delivery Chassis	$3580
F-6000 Chassis with Cab	$5710
F-6000 Stake Body (132-inch wb)	$6025
F-6000 Platform Body (132-inch wb)	$5950

C-6000 Tilt Cab with Chassis	$6700
N-6000 Chassis with Cab	$5755
N-6000 Stake Body (144-inch wb)	$6150
N-6000 Platform Body (144-inch wb)	$6050
B-6000 School Bus Chassis	$5310

1969

F-500 Chassis with Cab	$3275
F-500 Stake Body (132-inch wb)	$3580
F-500 Platform Body (132-inch wb)	$3515
F-500 Stake Body (156-inch wb)	$3635
F-500 Platform Body (156-inch wb)	$3540
N-500 Chassis with Cab	$3565
N-500 Stake Body (121-inch wb)	$3870
N-500 Platform Body (121-inch wb)	$3805
N-500 Stake Body (144-inch wb)	$3925
N-500 Platform Body (144-inch wb)	$3860
C-550 Chassis with Tilt Cab	$4450
B-500 School Bus Chassis	$3010
P-400 Parcel Delivery Chassis	$2225
P-500 Parcel Delivery Chassis	$2425
F-600 Chassis with Cab	$3520
N-600 Chassis with Cab	$3780
N-600 Stake Body (121-inch wb)	$4085
N-600 Platform Body (121-inch wb)	$4020
B-600 School Bus Chassis	$3270
F-6000 Chassis with Cab	$6275
F-6000 Stake Body (132-inch wb)	$6600
F-6000 Platform Body (132-inch wb)	$6525
N-6000 Chassis with Cab	$6300
C-6000 Chassis with Tilt Cab	$7225
B-6000 School Bus Chassis	$5770
P-4000 Parcel Delivery Chassis	$3310
P-5000 Parcel Delivery Chassis	$3580

1970

F-500 Chassis with Cab	$3540
LN-500 Chassis with Cab	$4175
B-500 School Bus Chassis	$3270
C-550 Chassis with Tilt Cab	$5030
P-400 Parcel Delivery Chassis	$2285
P-500 Parcel Delivery Chassis	$2915

F-600 Chassis with Cab	$3785
LN-600 Chassis with Cab	$4325
C-600 Chassis with Tilt Cab	$5115
B-600 School Bus Chassis	$3530
F-6000 Chassis with Cab	$6670
LN-6000 Chassis with Cab	$7260
C-6000 Chassis with Tilt Cab	$8045
B-6000 School Bus Chassis	$6185
P-4000 Parcel Delivery Chassis	$3260
P-5000 Parcel Delivery Chassis	$4160

1971

F-500 Chassis with Cab	$3988
LN-500 Chassis with Cab	$4418
C-550 Chassis with Tilt Cab	$5451
B-500 School Bus Chassis	$3816
P-400 Parcel Delivery Chassis	$2563
P-500 Parcel Delivery Chassis	$3281
F-600 Chassis with Cab	$4092
LN-600 Chassis with Cab	$4491
C-600 Chassis with Tilt Cab	$5570
F-600 4x4 Chassis with Cab	$7102
B-600 School Bus Chassis	$3932
F-6000 Chassis with Cab	$7343
LN-6000 Chassis with Cab	$7756
C-6000 Chassis with Tilt Cab	$8935
B-6000 School Bus Chassis	$7096
P-4000 Parcel Delivery Chassis	$3680
P-5000 Parcel Delivery Chassis	$4502

1972

F-500 Chassis with Cab	$4085
P-400 Parcel Delivery Chassis	$2455
P-500 Parcel Delivery Chassis	$3350
B-500 School Bus Chassis	$3910
F-600 Chassis with Cab	$4195
LN-600 Chassis with Cab	$4865
C-600 Chassis with Cab	$5620
F-600 4x4 Chassis with Cab	$7205
F-6000 Chassis with Cab	$7650
LN-6000 Chassis with Cab	$8075
C-6000 Chassis with Tilt Cab	$9285
B-6000 School Bus Chassis	$7400

Ford prepared and distributed this layout book to Ford truck salesmen and body builders. Inside there are technical drawings of all Ford truck chassis options for the 1973 model year. *John McLaughlin Collection*

Chapter 10: Some Improvements to an Already Popular Truck Line 1973-1979

The 1973 model year would see quite a few changes made to the Ford F Series line of trucks. First and foremost they were fitted with a redesigned cab. The cab was a bit longer this year to allow for more space behind the seat. That extra length provided for a little more legroom as well. These redesigned cabs were mated to some redesigned doors. The character line in the doors,

which bulged out on 1967 to 1972 models, was changed to a design that was more covelike; in other words it curved in rather than bulging out.

The front fenders of these trucks were redesigned too and now they looked to be a little narrower than the early front fenders. Besides these changes Ford also changed the design of the hood and they added larger F O R D letters to the face of these restyled hoods.

Flanking the hood, sitting atop the front fenders, the turn signal lamps were now of a square design rather than being round as they were before.

Another change seen on these restyled Ford F Series trucks was a new grille. This new grille was comprised of a series of horizontal bars combined with vertical bars. The previous grille treatment featured a center mounted vertical bar with five horizontal bars while the new grille was made up of three vertical bars along with four horizontal bars.

Once again Ford expanded their Medium-Duty Truck ranks this year to include the F-700, F-7000, and F-750 model trucks. Ford also decided to increase their participation this year in the manufacturing and supplying of even more chassis to the motor home industry. Ford started referring to this separate line of trucks as their "M Series," and four versions of this chassis were offered under a special order basis.

The lowest rated version of this M Chassis, the M-450, was available in wheelbase lengths of 137, 154, and 159 inches. The standard equipment engine for this chassis was Ford's 360 cubic inch V-8, which was mated to a Ford 3-speed C-6 Cruise-O-Matic transmission and a Rockwell C-100 rear axle with a 4.33:1 ratio. If a more powerful engine was needed Ford offered their 390 cubic inch V-8 as an option in this chassis.

If buyers wanted a heavier-duty rated motor home chassis Ford offered their M-500 Chassis which was available in three versions. The lowest rated M-500 was the M-502 which had a GVW rating of 12,000 lbs. Next up was the M-504 which had a GVW rating of 12,800 lbs. And finally there was the M-505, which carried a GVW rating of 15,000 lbs.

The M-500 Chassis was available with wheelbases of 137, 154, 159, and 178 inches. Like the lower rated M-450 Chassis the frames on these chassis layouts were of a single channel design. However, both the M-450 and the M-500s used

The Venice Fire Department of Venice, Illinois, is where you will find this 1973 Ford F-600 fire truck with a McCabe-Powers rescue body. *Dennis J. Maag*

We found this Ford F-600 truck sitting on a farm in Kansas. The reason why it sits so high is that it is one of Ford's 4x4 models.

different frames depending on their wheelbase lengths. The 137-inch wheelbase models used a steel frame with a 6.24-inch section modulus while the longer wheelbase models used a stronger frame with a 9.45-inch section modulus.

The M-500 models came with a 390 cubic inch

Back in 1976 your author drove a Ford F-600 moving van like this one shown here to move his household goods from one end of the country to the other.

V-8 engine as standard equipment. Like the M-450 that engine was mated to a Ford C-6 Cruise-O-Matic transmission. A stronger rear end, the Rockwell D-100, was fitted to these trucks and it carried a rear end ratio of 5.29:1 as standard equipment. Three other axles were offered as options on the M-500 Chassis. One was a Rockwell D-100 with a 5.83:1 rear axle ratio while the other two were Rockwell F-106s with gear ratios of 6.2:1 and 6.8:1.

The F Series and B Series Ford trucks for the 1974 model year were treated to a few upgrades. The major change on the F-6000 and the B-6000 was the addition of a heavier-duty rated 6,000-lb. capacity front axle that replaced a lighter-duty axle used on the 1973 models. Minor changes could be seen in the interior trimmings found in the F Series and L Series of trucks as well.

Ford's Tilt Cab trucks, otherwise known as their C Series line, were still the most popular trucks of their kind in the United States. This year, for the first time in many years, the C Series Ford trucks were treated to a design change. The cab design stayed the same but the wheel well lips were widened so they now stood out from the sides of the cab.

Another new option for the C-600 trucks was the availability of a C-6 3-speed Cruise-O-Matic transmission as an extra cost option.

Though it doesn't look like it, this 1974 Ford C Series Tilt Cab truck has been in service for more than 30 years.

Ford was still heavily involved in the motor home chassis business with their M Series of chassis. A new addition to the M-450 Series this year was a shorter, 125-inch wheelbase model. Also for those who wanted a more powerful engine in one of these chassis Ford offered their 460 cubic inch V-8 engine as an option.

The 1975 model year would see a number of changes, both minor and major in nature, to Ford's medium-duty trucks. The major changes involved Ford's gasoline engines, which were upgraded with piston and cooling system changes. Ford also changed the name of their heavy-duty truck engines this year. Before this change they were referred to as Heavy-Duty or "HD" engines. Now Ford changed that terminology and called them "Extra-Duty" or "XD" for short. They also listed new cubic inch displacements for 360 and 390 cubic inch engines in their medium-duty trucks. The 360 became the 361 and the 390 became the 391. Ford took this step to help differentiate these motors from the light-duty 360 and 390 cubic inch V-8s that were available as options in lighter-duty F Series trucks in 1975.

A minor change seen on the C Series of Ford trucks this year was the deletion of the Ford truck "gear and thunderbolt" crest seen on the front ends of these trucks since 1957.

In our bicentennial year of 1976 Ford again made a number of changes to all their trucks. For medium-duty F-600 buyers Ford offered a new, four-door, six-man Crew Cab option, which was a perfect solution for truck buyers who needed to carry extra men. This Crew Cab option was only available on 2-wheel-drive models of the F-600. For those who wanted a 4x4 version of the F-600 it was still available with a 330 cubic inch "Extra-Duty" V-8 engine, a 4-speed manual transmission, and a 2-speed transfer case.

Ford's F Series medium-duty trucks this year also featured new steering boxes and some new manual transmissions were also added to their option lists.

This Ford L Series bottling truck waits for another load of soda pop to deliver to stores around the Albuquerque area.

A short wheelbase Ford L Series dump truck sits parked on a residential street outside a construction project in Arlington, Massachusetts, back in the late 1980s.

A Ford Parcel Delivery Chassis, probably a P-500, sits under this Gerstenslager Rescue Body which served the Madison, Illinois, area before it was retired in 2002 and offered for sale. *Dennis J. Maag*

1977 was another year for changes for Ford's Truck Division. Chief among these changes were some consolidations of model lines as well as dropping some model lines.

At the beginning of the model year the F-500 was still Ford's base model line in their Medium-Duty rated ranks, however, due to declining sales and demand Ford dropped the F-500 from their catalogs halfway through the model year. Also dropped around the same time were Ford's P Series Parcel Delivery Chassis models and their Motor Home Chassis (M-Series) of trucks.

Ford also took this opportunity to consolidate their F-700 and F-750 series of trucks. Ford combined the two into a new F-700 Series, which had higher GVW ratings. Other changes seen included new rear end and transmission selections.

On July 27, 1977, Ford's Truck Division celebrated the "60th Anniversary" of the Ford Motor Company getting involved in the truck business in 1917 with their introduction of the Model TT trucks. Later on in the year they also celebrated the fact that Ford trucks were the number one selling trucks in the world with over 1,214,000 units being sold in the 1977 model year.

The Ford Motor Company celebrated another anniversary in 1978. It was their "75th Anniversary" of the founding of the company by Henry Ford

Another Ford F-600 4x4 truck sits at a gas drilling site in Southern Colorado. Its high ground clearance allows it to practically go anywhere to do its job.

on June 16, 1903. Soon after the start of the 1978 model year, which began around October of 1977, they celebrated the production of a special vehicle that was built in their Mahwah, New Jersey, plant on November 15. This special vehicle, a 1978 Fairmont Futura, was the "100 Millionth" vehicle that Ford had built since 1903. What made this event even more special was the fact that this unique vehicle was also one of the new vehicles that Ford had introduced in this model year. Joining the Fairmont was a new Mercury Zephyr that was based on the same platform, a new larger sized Bronco Utility Vehicle, and some new Econoline models.

In heavy truck news at Ford the major story

revolved around Ford's release of a new line hauler premium extra heavy-duty truck to replace their "W" Series trucks. This new model was called the CL-9000 and it was quite an impressive looking and performing truck. Like the "W" Series before it this truck was designed to compete against the likes of Peterbilts, Kenworths, Marmons, and other Class 8 trucks. Ford's new CL-9000 compared favorably to all of them.

With all this money going to developing, releasing, and producing all these new Ford vehicles there was hardly any money left over to improve Ford's medium-duty and heavy-duty trucks this year. However, if buyers wanted an

This Ford promotional postcard showing a Ford F-600 farm truck in action was used to promote a Ford "Custom Special Sale."

rior. Ford also offered a similar tape treatment for their larger heavy-duty trucks that they called an "Owner/Operator Package."

Though they looked the same on the outside as the 1978 models Ford made a number of improvements to their medium-duty trucks this year. For 1979 Ford fitted these trucks with maintenance-free batteries and plastic fender inner liners to cut down on corrosion. They also gave them a smoother ride thanks to a new wheel-balancing program at the factory.

Replacing the 361 and 391 cubic inch V-8 gasoline engines this year were some new engines that Ford referred to as their "Lima V-8s." That name was given to them because they were built in the Ford engine facility in Lima, Ohio.

The smallest of these new "Lima V-8s" was an engine that displaced 370 cubic inches. This 370 cubic inch V-8 was available in two forms. One used a 2-barrel carburetor while the other used a 4-barrel carburetor. For buyers who needed a truck with a bigger gasoline V-8 Ford offered the "Lima" 429 cubic inch V-8. Both engines put out more power than the 361 and 391 cubic inch V-8s they replaced and they turned in better gas mileage figures.

F-600 or an F-700 this year and wanted it to look different than other similar trucks Ford offered a new "Exterior Tape Dress Up Package" as an option on these trucks. This was no ordinary tape package with small strips of tape to dress up the truck. The tape supplied in these kits were big pieces, which when applied to the cabs and fenders of these trucks made them look like a two-tone paint finish had been applied to the exte-

Another Ford promotional postcard advertising a "Ford Custom Special Sale." Note that all the models shown on this postcard are equipped with "Custom" equipment.

The owner of these Boss 429 Mustangs uses this 1976 Ford F-600 ex-U-Haul ramp truck to haul these cars to shows around the country.

Diesel engine-equipped models like the F-7000 and the LN-7000 are powered this year by Caterpillar V636 engines that have horsepower ratings of 175. Optional Caterpillar V636 engines for these trucks carried horsepower ratings of 200 and 210.

Looking back over the years that transpired during this part of the 1970s decade we can see that Ford did well in all the market segments it competed in. Their "Louisville Line" set the standard at the start of the decade for medium and heavy-duty trucks. And the public responded quite favorably to all of Ford's car and truck offerings, which helped to keep the Ford Motor Company at the top of the sales charts year in and year out. In the car and truck business things don't get any better than that.

Another Ford that lost its "R" making it a "FOD." This L Series Ford service truck is equipped with the Custom Cab option with its bright finished grille and windshield trim band.

Chapter 11: Aerodynamics Leading the Way — The 1980s

Once again the 1980s would be a decade that saw lots of changes for Ford's trucks. Leading those changes was a new aerodynamic restyling job done on Ford's F Series trucks. Ford called these trucks their "Job Tough" trucks and they had the looks to back up that claim. With their large, wide-mouthed grilles and muscular looking swept-back front fenders they certainly looked the part of tough trucks.

Ford's F Series heavy, medium-duty, and higher rated trucks featured new larger, more comfortable cabs. Those cabs were mated with redesigned doors, hoods, and fiberglass front fenders. A fiber-

glass grille panel surround housed a wide two-piece plastic grille that was separated by a set of F O R D letters. The steel cabs on these trucks were immersed in a high voltage charged primer dip bath to help cut down on rust corrosion.

The new cabs were mounted on new stronger frames, which were available with nine different wheelbase lengths in the Medium-Duty range. Ford also offered their medium-duty truck buyers a choice of 14 transmissions and 11 rear axle setups.

Other improvements noted for the 1980 Ford F Series trucks were an integral climate-controlled air system and improved electrical systems and connections. These F Series trucks also came with redesigned interiors in three levels of trim. The first was the "Standard Level," the mid range was the "Custom Level," and the really deluxe version was the "Custom Hi-Level."

In July of 1980 the Ford Motor Company announced that in addition to their gasoline and diesel fueled vehicles they were going to offer their customers another choice in what fuel to use. This new fuel option was known as Liquid Petroleum Gas, or LPG, for short. You might know of LPG by another name — propane.

The benefits of using propane are that it burns cleaner than gasoline or diesel fuel so it is less polluting. Cleaner running engines also require less maintenance thereby reducing costs. Cleaner running engines also tend to last longer further reducing costs. Another plus for using propane is that it can cut down on our dependence on foreign oil supplies.

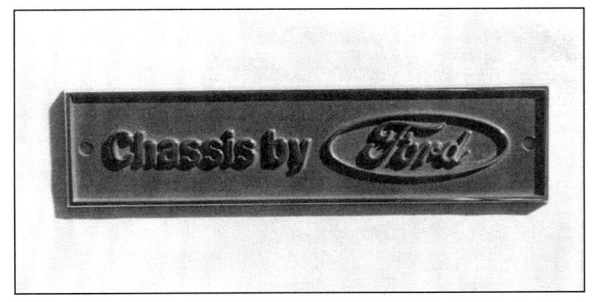

This plate was attached to the front ends of Ford Parcel Delivery and Motor Home Chassis back in the 1980s.

Ford offered this LPG option on its 370 and 429 cubic inch Lima gasoline V-8 engines. These engines were modified at the factory and came complete with Ford warranties — warranties that were not offered by aftermarket LPG converters or other manufacturers. Ford's modifications

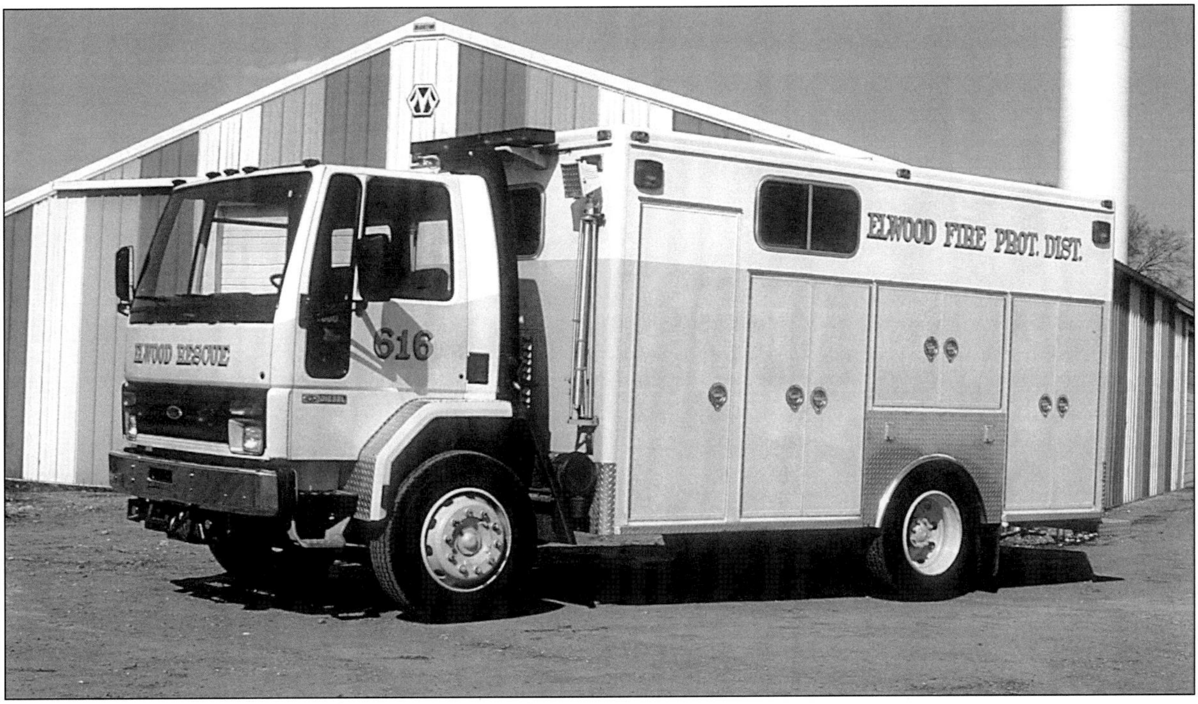

Here we see a 1986 Ford Cargo truck fitted with a McCoy-Miller Rescue Body. It is used by the Elwood Fire Protection District of Elwood, Illinois. *Dennis J. Maag*

This Ford F Series truck has been outfitted for tractor-trailer work. Notice the sleeper on the back of the cab.

This Ford F Series truck has been fitted with a roll back tow truck service body. Tag on lower left of its grille shows that it is powered by a 370-cubic-inch Lima V-8 engine.

consisted of recalibrating the distributor to better match the distributor to the most efficient LPG power advance curve. The intake manifold on these engines was also modified to meet the lower operating temperatures required by the use of propane. Special cylinder heads with hard-faced alloy valve seat inserts were also used on these engines. Non-chrome-plated piston rings were specified for use to help minimize ring-seating problems that can be associated with the use of LPG. Use of chrome-plated piston rings in this application can result in excessive oil consumption.

Ford's Factory LPG Option Parts
6.1L 370 Cubic Inch 4V V-8 Engine
7.0L 429 Cubic Inch 4V V-8 Engine
Impco Model VFF-30 Filter Fuelock
Impco Model EOS-20 Converter
Impco CAG-425-20 4V Carburetor with Electronic Governor
Special Fuel Tank with Associated Hardware
LPG Air Cleaner Setup
Special Instrument Cluster which replaces the Gasoline Gauge
All Gasoline Engine Emission Equipment Deleted
Non-Chrome-Plated Piston Rings
Modified Intake Manifold
Special 10-Degree Lower Operating Thermostat

How Ford's LPG System Works
The propane fuel comes from its storage tank and is drawn into the filter fuelock. This filter fuelock serves two functions. Its primary function is to keep solid contaminants in the fuel from reaching the carburetor. While its secondary function is to regulate the flow of fuel from the tank to the converter. It also shuts off the flow of fuel to the carburetor when the engine is shut off. It does this through the use of a manifold pressure-actuated control valve.

The next part of the system is the converter,

which changes the liquefied petroleum gas from the fuel tank into a vapor mist that can be transferred to the carburetor. Engine coolant, which is warm, is circulated through the coolant passages in this converter to help counteract the refrigerating effect of the expanding propane fuel. This converter is of a two-stage design because it uses two pressure seats to regulate the pressure in the system. One is a high-pressure seat while the other is a low-pressure seat. The high-pressure seat reduces the pressure of the fuel coming from the tank while the low-pressure seat lowers the pressure even further until it reaches the right pressure for entry into the carburetor fuel inlets. This converter also uses an engine vacuum-actuated control valve, which shuts off fuel when the engine is turned off.

Like gasoline fueled Ford engines of the time these LPG modified engines used a carburetor to mix the fuel with air. However, this carburetor was a bit different. The carburetor used with this LPG setup is called an "Air-Valve" carburetor and like a regular gasoline carburetor airflow into the engine is controlled by a butterfly valve in the carburetor's venturi. As air is drawn in a pressure change is created in the venturi. That pressure change causes a diaphragm at the top of the carburetor to move up and down. Attached to that diaphragm is a fuel metering valve and a measuring valve, which opens and closes as that diaphragm moves up and down. Those valves assure that the proper air/fuel mixture is fed into the engine at just the right time so that it runs at its most efficient state under all situations and speeds.

For 1981 the F Series trucks looked the same as the previous 1980 models. Engine choices this year for the F-600 trucks included the 6.1L, 370 cubic inch 2V V-8 as standard equipment with the 6.1L, 370 cubic inch 4V V-8 as an option. Diesel truck buyers could also order an 8.2L, 500 cubic inch, normally aspirated Detroit Diesel "Fuel Pincher" V-8 engine as an option. If none of these engines fit the bill buyers could also choose a Ford

Ford released their new Cargo trucks here in the USA in 1986. Shown here is a picture of the 1987 Cargo catalog.

A couple of new Ford F Series Nynex cable repair trucks are shown working on a cable repair job after a snowstorm in New England back in the late 1980s.

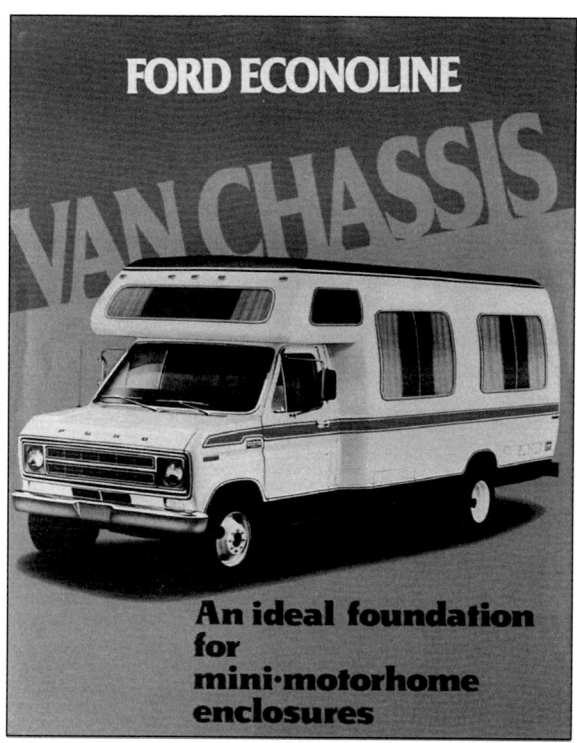

This Ford F-600 Crew Cab truck with a platform body is an ex-New York Highway Department truck.

This catalog covers equipment found on Ford's Econoline Van Chassis models. Some of these chassis models had GVW ratings that put them into the lower medium-duty range.

LPG engine option as well.

F-700 trucks on the other hand came with a 6.1L 370 cubic inch 4V V-8 engine as standard equipment with a 6.1L, 370 cubic inch 2V V-8 engine as an option. Or buyers could order a truck with a 7.0L (429 cubic inch) 4V V-8 engine for a powerplant. If diesel engines were desired in an F-700 Ford truck this year Ford offered the choice of two 8.2L, 500 cubic inch, Detroit Diesel V-8 engines from which to choose. One was normally aspirated while the other was turbocharged. Both were also listed as options in Ford's LN-700 and C-700 trucks as well. You could also get a normally aspirated Detroit Diesel V-8 engine in the

C-600 and LN-600 models.

Both the F-600 and F-700 series of trucks came with a New Process 435 4-speed direct manual transmission as standard equipment. Optional transmissions for these trucks included the following:

Warner T-19 4-Speed Direct
Clark 282V 5-Speed Direct
Clark 285V 5-Speed Direct
Clark 282 VHD 5-Speed Direct Heavy-Duty
Clark 285 VHD 5-Speed Direct Heavy-Duty
New Process 542 HD 5-Speed Direct Heavy-Duty
New Process 542 FL 5-Speed Direct
Clark 390V 5-Speed Direct (F-700)
Clark 397V 5-Speed Direct (F-700)
Spicer 5052A 5-Speed Direct
Spicer 5252A 5-Speed Direct
Allison AT545 4-Speed Automatic
Allison AT643 4-Speed Automatic

Once again this year Ford's F Series trucks were available in three levels. And even the base Standard Trim Level was pretty impressive. Below is a listing of what came with each interior trim type.

Standard Level Trim

All vinyl seat trim in blue, red, or brown
5 inches of foam padding in seat
Color-keyed Door Panels
Armrests with integral door handles
Reversible Key Locks
Deluxe Instrument Panel
Glove box with integrated coin slots and cup depressions
Ashtray
Coat hook
Left sun visor
Bright metal windshield band
2-speed electric windshield wipers

Custom Trim

In addition to items already mentioned in the Standard Level:
Breathable custom knitted vinyl seat coverings in red, blue, or brown
Brushed aluminum instrument panel appliqué
Deluxe sound and heat insulation
Cigarette Lighter
Right-hand sun visor
Color-keyed door panels with bright moldings

Hi-Level Trim

In addition to items in Standard and Custom Levels:
Color-keyed door panels with brushed aluminum insert and carpeting on lower areas
Color-keyed headliner trim
Color-keyed cut pile carpeting
Color-keyed garnish moldings
Color-keyed polyknit vinyl seat covers in blue or red

Other changes noted on 1981 Ford trucks included the C Series Tilt Cabs getting a 30-gallon fuel tank and a 920 cubic inch vacuum reserve tank as standard equipment. Fuel lines in the F Series trucks were re-routed to the outside of the frame rails to help isolate these lines from high

"F-600 Diesel" cowl badge as used on late 1980s Ford F Series trucks that used Ford diesel engines.

Center Ford, of Center, Colorado, uses this F-600 tow truck as a service truck to take care of their customer's in that area.

engine temperatures to help minimize vapor lock situations.

For the first time in Ford truck history steel belted radial tires were offered as an option to help increase

The Santa Fe/Burlington North Rail Road uses this F-700 Ford truck with a stake body to service their rails in the Southern Colorado area.

fuel economy and to make these trucks handle better. If you wanted to dress up the exterior looks of your F Series truck Ford offered a new Exterior Multi-Tone Tape Package (pin stripes) that accentuated the lines of the cab, hood, and front fenders.

For 1982 a new Ford F-700 4x4 truck model was offered for buyers who needed a heavier-duty truck to take off-road. F-600 trucks with long 225- or 237-inch wheelbases were fitted with frames that were rated at 50,000 psi as standard equipment. This was the same rated frame that was used on F-700 and F-800 trucks this year.

For buyers of LN-7000 trucks the standard engine this year was a Caterpillar 3208 diesel V-8 rated at 175 horsepower. Three other Caterpillar 3208 engines were offered as options with horse-power ratings of 165,185, and 200.

Buyers who were looking for a less costly medium-duty Ford truck this year could opt for a "Stripped Chassis" model. This "Stripped Chassis" model was available as either an LN-600 or an LN-700 truck. Either one was available with a 6.1L 370 cubic inch Lima 2V V-8 or a new, lower powered (130 hp) version of the 8.2L Detroit Diesel V-8.

Ford still listed the B-600 and B-700 School Bus Chassis in their catalogs during 1982. The B-600 was available in the following chassis wheel-base lengths:

151-inch wheelbase for 36 passengers
193-inch wheelbase for 48 passengers
217-inch wheelbase for 54 passengers
237-inch wheelbase for 60 passengers

The B-700 was available in one of the following wheelbases:

237-inch wheelbase for 60 passengers
255-inch wheelbase for 66 passengers
275-inch wheelbase for 72 passengers

As before all Ford medium-duty trucks were offered with gasoline, diesel, or LPG fueled engines this year. And to improve their headlight systems all trucks were fitted with halogen headlamps this year.

For the 1983 model year the Ford F Series truck line was expanded to cover new F-7000 and F-8000 models in single and tandem rear axle arrangements.

These new Ford diesel engine models were available with Caterpillar 3208 V-8 engines as standard equipment. The 3208NA engine was a normally aspirated diesel V-8 that was designed to run in mid-range applications like in city, suburban, or local rural service. These engines displaced 10.4L or 636 cubic inches and were rated at 165,175, and 200 with maximum torque ratings of 455, 415, and 470 ft/lbs at 1,200 to 1,400 rpm. After February of 1983 a new 3208T (T for turbocharged) Caterpillar V-8 engine rated at 210 horsepower at 2,600 rpm with a maximum torque rating of 550 ft/lbs at 1,400 rpm was made available in F-7000, F-8000, C-7000, C-8000, CT-8000, L-8000, and LT-8000 models as another option. All these Caterpillar 3208 engines could be had with 5- or 10-speed manual transmissions.

If you didn't want to pay a premium price for a Ford truck with a Caterpillar engine in your medium-duty truck you could opt for a "Fuel Pincher" Detroit Diesel engine in any truck in the F, C, B, or L Series.

"Quality Is Job 1" was the new theme at the Ford Motor Company for 1984. Ford employees, from upper management all the way down to the assembly line worker, joined together to discuss ways of improving their products and the way they were assembled. Their goal was to build the best quality vehicle they could before it was delivered to the customer.

The big news concerning Ford trucks this year was the release of a new advanced braking system for their medium-duty trucks. This new split system offered the truck buyer a system that offered an air brake system at a price normally associated with a hydraulic system.

This new system powered by hydraulic pressure was operable as soon as the engine was started so you didn't need to wait until air pressure built up in the system before you could drive off. At the front of this system was a set of fade resistant front disc brakes with semi-metallic linings on the pads

This good-looking Ford L Series dump truck was found on a used truck lot in Minneapolis, Minnesota, in the late 1990s.

for longer wear. Out back the rear brake drums were designed to run cooler to minimize brake system fade. The shoes in these brake drums featured 3/4-inch-thick linings.

Another feature of this new braking system was a spring loaded parking brake. This brake was set with a push/pull control knob like on air brake systems. This new parking brake system did away with the usual driveline parking brake.

Hydraulic pressure for these brakes was supplied by a hydraulic pump, which fed a dual master cylinder and a booster. This system did away with the vacuum booster, reserve take, and lines usually associated with air brake systems. As an added safety bonus of this system the booster had a back up electric motor and if the system failed for any reason this motor was activated. When that happened a warning light and buzzer warned the driver of a brake problem.

In 1985 Ford's F Series trucks received a new grille design with a new Ford oval crest that sepa-

This used Ford L Series truck has been dressed up a bit with a chrome plated front bumper and a new construction type body.

rated the upper and lower portions on the grille and replaced the F O R D letters.

Another new Ford F Series option this year was the availability of a one-piece fiberglass tilting front end option in addition to the regular standard front end setup of a normal hood, grille, and separate front fenders. This tilting option allowed the whole front-end unit to tilt forward, which made access to the engine a whole lot simpler.

Also getting new Ford oval emblems this year were the C and L Series of trucks.

The year 1986 brought another all new model into the Ford truck lineup. This new model was

called the Cargo. Ford called it "A Tough New Truck From America's Medium Truck Leader." Though new to the USA market this year the Cargo had been introduced to the European truck market in 1981. The Cargo had five full years of road testing before it came to U.S. shores.

The Cargo was a Tilt Cab truck with contemporary European styling cues. It was designed and first built in England but the Cargo destined for sale in the North American and Latin American markets was built in Ford's Ipiranga Truck Plant in Sao Paulo, Brazil, and imported into this country through the port of Baltimore. Ford offered the

A Ford F-600 truck at a job site is shown servicing a Caterpillar front end loader in this photograph. It carries gasoline, diesel fuel, oil, and all sorts of lubricants.

Cargo in a 6000 and a 7000 Series. These trucks were also offered in 153-, 171-, and 189-inch wheelbase lengths.

Power was supplied by a turbocharged Ford in-line 6-cylinder diesel engine that had a maximum horsepower rating of 165 at 2,600 rpm.

Ford Diesel Engine Specifications
In-line 6-Cylinder LayoutGarrett Turbocharger
Direct Injection Fuel System
Bore and Stroke: 4.4 x 4.4
Displacement: 6.6L or 401 cubic inches
Maximum Gross Horsepower: 165 at 2,600 rpm
Maximum Gross Torque: (49 States) 388 ft/lbs at 1,600 rpm
 (California) 410 ft/lbs at 1,800 rpm
Compression Ratio: 17.0 to 1

Engine Mounting: 3-point rubber insulated
Governor: Bosch
Governor Type: Full range mechanical
Injectors: Bosch

Ford offered two transmissions as an option with these Cargo trucks — a 5-speed direct manual or a 4-speed automatic.

The cabs on these trucks had a futuristic aerodynamic look to them. They had lots of glass areas including a large windshield and lots of window glass areas in their doors. These cabs could be tilted up to a full 50 degrees to provide easy access for maintenance on the engine and transmission. As an added bonus a panel on the front of the cab was easily removable to check fluid levels. If required the plastic grille could be removed for repairs to

This Ford F Series Crew Cab truck now owned by a construction company in New Mexico was originally owned by the Texas State Highway Department. It was used as a highway crew service truck.

wiring or equipment in the front part of the cab.

Inside the driver and his passengers were treated to a comfortable, spacious, world-class environment. This 3-person cab featured comfortable contoured seats, a large two-spoke steering wheel, easy to read gauges and easy to reach controls, and a fresh air system that recycled cab air every 20 seconds. Talk about state of the art!

Ford even offered buyers of these Cargo trucks their choice of 22 easy to order "Work-Ready" Cargo trucks with specific equipment already installed on them. All a buyer had to do was sit down and have a truck salesman fill out the "Work-Ready" order form. For example, a model number "6000-601" order got a buyer a Cargo 6000 Series

truck on a 153-inch wheelbase chassis with a 4-speed automatic transmission, single speed rear axle, hydraulic brakes, and an engine shutdown system. Or if he ordered a model number "7000-608" he received a Cargo 7000 Series truck on a 189-inch wheelbase chassis with a 5-speed manual transmission, a two-speed rear axle, air brakes, and an engine shutdown system.

Now Ford had two Tilt Cab trucks in their lineup — this new Cargo and the tried and true C Series Tilt Cabs.

The already mentioned Ford "Work-Ready" Truck Program was made available this year to other Ford trucks besides the Cargo Tilt Cab truck. Ford even went so far as to tailor make these "Work-Ready" trucks for specific jobs for the refuse industry, jobs for the construction industry, jobs that required tractor-trailer rigs, and jobs that required a van, stake, or platform body. Here are some examples of the "Work-Ready" codes that were used and how they decoded:

F-700-634: A truck designed for refuse work. Under that code the truck was an F-700 with a conventional cab and a GVW rating of 28,000 lbs on a 189-inch wheelbase chassis. A Ford gasoline engine with a 5-speed manual transmission and a 2-speed rear axle rated at 19,000 lbs supplied power.

F-600-606: A truck designed for construction work. The truck was an F-600 with a conventional cab with a GVW rating of 21,000 lbs on a 141-inch wheelbase chassis. A Ford gasoline engine with a 5-speed manual transmission and a 2-speed rear axle rated at 15,000 lbs supplied power.

F-800-615: A trailer truck model. This was an F-800 with a conventional cab and a GVW rating of 55,000 lbs. This truck sat on a 141-inch wheelbase chassis. A Detroit Diesel V-8 engine mated to a 5-speed manual transmission supplied power. A 9000 lb rated axle was on the front of this truck while a 19,000 lb rated 2-speed rear axle was on the back of it.

As you can see with these examples Ford made it relatively easy to order a truck that was already equipped with specific parts. By using this system a buyer could get his truck a lot faster than through a regular ordering process because a lot of these trucks were already built and sitting in Ford's "Work-Ready" area lot at their Kentucky Truck Plant. If the truck weren't already built Ford would guarantee that the truck could be built and delivered in less than 45 days. As an added bonus to use this "Work-Ready" program for ordering a truck Ford offered an "Extended Service Coverage" warranty at no extra charge. This warranty was in addition to the regular warranty Ford offered on their trucks.

If you still wanted to spec out your own truck you could do so by placing a regular order through your local Ford dealer.

Ford's 1987 truck promotional campaign was set around the theme that these new Ford trucks were "An Investment In Value" because of all the extras that came with these trucks at no extra charge. This was sort of like a modern day rendition of the "Bonus Built" campaign of the late 1940s and early 1950s. Ford's C Series Tilt Cab trucks celebrated being in service for 30 years but now the C Series line was down to just three models. The lowest rated C Series truck this year was the C-800, which came with a Detroit Diesel V-8 engine. The C-8000 and the CT-8000, the other two C Series models, were available with Caterpillar 3208 diesel engines. If buyers wanted a lower rated tilt cab they were shown a Cargo 6000 or Cargo 7000 truck.

Ford was still in the School Bus Chassis business in 1987 with their B-600, B-700, and B-7000 models. The standard engine in the B-600 was still the Lima 6.1L (370 cubic inch) gasoline V-8. Optional engines for this model included a 6.1L (370 cubic inch) 4V V-8, an 8.2L (500 cubic inch) Detroit Diesel V-8, and a 6.6L (401 cubic inch) Turbocharged Ford in-line 6-cylinder Diesel engine.

The standard engine for the B-700 Series was also a 6.1L (370 cubic inch) 2V Lima V-8. Optional engines for the B-700 included the following:
6.1L (370 cubic inch) 4V Lima V-8
7.0L (429 cubic inch) 4V Lima V-8
8.2L (500 cubic inch) Detroit Diesel V-8 165 horsepower
8.2L (500 cubic inch) Detroit Diesel Turbocharged V-8 200 horsepower (for California)
8.2L (500 cubic inch) Detroit Diesel V-8 Turbocharged 205 horsepower
6.6L (401 cubic inch) Turbocharged In-line Ford 6-cylinder Diesel 170 horsepower
7.8L (474 cubic inch) Turbocharged In-line Ford 6-cylinder Diesel 185 horsepower

7.8L (474 cubic inch) Turbocharged In-line Ford 6-cylinder Diesel 210 horsepower

The standard engine for the B-7000 Series School Bus Chassis was a Caterpillar 3208NA Diesel V-8 with a horsepower rating of 165. Optional engines for this bus series were the 3208 engines with horsepower ratings of 175 and 200.

All B Series School Bus Chassis featured full channel frames made out of hi-tensile steel. They also came with power steering at no extra charge and for those bus operators who wanted a one-piece fiberglass tilting front end this year Ford offered one as an option on their B Series buses.

In 1987 Ford claimed that their Cargo trucks were now their fastest growing medium-duty trucks. Ford referred to these trucks as their "low-tilt" models to differentiate them from their "high-tilt" regular C Series Tilt Cabs.

Ford's Cargo trucks now came with a choice of three Ford diesel truck engines. The smallest of the three was the Turbocharged 6.6L (401 cubic inch) in-line 6-cylinder engine, which now had a gross horsepower rating of 170 at 2,600 rpm. This engine also produced 402 ft/lbs of torque (maximum) at 1,600 rpm.

The next engine up the power ladder was Ford's 7.8L (474 cubic inch) Turbocharged in-line 6-cylinder diesel with a horsepower rating of 185 (gross) at 2,600 rpm. This engine also had a gross torque rating of 467 ft/lbs at 1,600 rpm.

And at the top of the power heap was Ford's 7.8L (474 cubic inch) Turbocharged in-line 6-cylinder with a gross horsepower rating of 210 at 2,600 rpm. The gross torque rating of this engine was 509 ft/lbs at 1,600 rpm (not available in California).

For those customers who wanted a "Work-Ready" Cargo truck this year Ford increased the number of these truck models from 22 (1986) to over 100 different units for 1987.

Ford started to build some of their medium-duty trucks at the Kentucky Truck Plant this year

and for customers who wanted to buy an F Series "Work-Ready" truck Ford offered 122 different models of them to choose from.

Before the start of the 1988 model year Ford informed their dealers and truck salesmen that some of their models were going to be dropped. Since Ford wasn't going to offer the Caterpillar 3208 engine anymore in their medium-duty trucks the F-7000, F-8000, and FT-8000 models would be discontinued. Also being discontinued was the B-7000, which also used a Caterpillar 3208 engine previously.

Ford also announced at the same time that they were going to replace the Detroit Diesel engines in their trucks with their own Ford Diesel engines. That decision meant that the C-800 Tilt Cab model was also being discontinued.

Another announcement by Ford concerned their new series of Ford Super-Duty Chassis and Cab trucks. These Super-Duty trucks with their 14,500 lb GVW ratings were meant to fit between their regular "one-ton" trucks and their F-600 medium-duty trucks. Sort of like the F-4 "Bonus Built" trucks of an earlier decade. So I guess you could call these trucks "lighter medium-duty" units. Base engine for these trucks was a 7.5L (460 cubic inch) gasoline V-8. A 7.3L diesel engine was offered as an option. These trucks were also fitted with heavy-duty axles and springs as well.

To better combat the ravages of rust and corrosion Ford's F Series cabs, hood inner panel, floor pan, roof, running boards, back of cab panels, and outer cab panels were now pressed out of galvanized steel. The B Series School Bus Chassis also got cowl, hood, and floor panels pressed from galvanized steel.

Other Ford news this year concerned their rear axle supplier. Rockwell was named Ford's sole supplier for axles for their medium and heavy-duty trucks under Ford's Premium Supplier Team program.

Also announced at the same time was that the

Bendix "S Cam" air brake system would replace Rockwell air brake systems in Ford F-700, F-800, LN-7000, and LN-8000 trucks.

Ford additionally announced that some of their diesel engines would have higher horsepower ratings. These Ford Diesel engines were now rated at 160, 170, 185, and 210 horsepower in medium-duty truck applications. Beginning in January of 1988 a new Ford Diesel engine featuring an air-to-air intercooler would be available as an option. This one would carry a horsepower rating of 215.

This year Ford opened a plant in Baltimore near the port where the Cargo trucks came into the United States. This plant, which they called the "Cargo Modification Center," was opened so that Ford workers could install such equipment as air conditioning, an air dryer, an engine block heater, ether cold starting system, CB radio "hot" jacks, AM/FM radios, and white wheel paint. This plant also took care of pre-delivery preparation.

Ford made some improvements to their painting process at their Kentucky Truck Plant this year to give their trucks better paint jobs. A stainless steel roof was installed over the phosphate machine to keep out dirt and debris. This change allowed the truck cabs to come out cleaner with fewer residues that might contaminate other painting processes in the plant.

The plant's electrocoating tank was enlarged to provide more dunk time for immersed cabs. The circulation and filtration systems were also improved, which resulted in a better priming process. A new sanding booth, a new paint prep booth, and a better baking oven combined to produce better quality paint finishes on the exteriors of these trucks.

The L Series Ford trucks received a new grille treatment this year that consisted of a series of horizontal grille bars that replaced the honeycomb style of the earlier trucks. This new grille treatment featured a wide horizontal bar in the middle of the grille that held a Ford oval grille badge. Besides having a new grille outside the L Series featured a new Custom Hi-Level Interior Trim Option. This option included new seat covers with contrasting polyknit fabrics and fresh stitching patterns and seat cushion contours. Door trim panels were also changed with their upper portions now covered with a combination of vinyl and polyknit fabrics. The headliner in this option was also changed. Now the headliner had a polyknit fabric insert and a new embossed design. These trucks also came with a new combination dome and map reading light and new entry assist handles. Last but not least Ford announced the availability of a driver controlled locking rear axle setup on F-700 and F-800 trucks with air brakes and Rockwell RS-21-145 or Rockwell RS-23-160 single speed rear axles.

With all the changes seen on the 1988 Ford trucks changes to the 1989 models, if any, were minor in nature.

As you can see Ford made a number of changes to their truck lineups during this decade. They cut back in some model lines and they introduced a new model to the U.S. market with the introduction of their new Cargo models. In response to rising fuel costs they redesigned their trucks with aerodynamic styling touches to cut down on wind resistance. They offered more diesel engines to the mix to help increase fuel economy numbers. Let us not forget their introduction of LPG fueled trucks to help clean up our environment as well as trying to help decrease our dependence on foreign oil supplies. Taking that all into consideration you have to agree it was a good decade to go with Ford trucks.

This photograph shows a Ford Cargo CF-7000 equipped with a long box-type van body.

Chapter 12: What Is Going On Here — The 1990s

Ford began the 1990s with the same truck models available that they had when the decade ended with the last of the 1989 models being produced. Now they called their trucks their "Work Force" models and this "Work Force" lineup team included Ford's F Series, B Series, C Series, L Series, and their Cargo trucks.

This little chart (opposite) will show you what F Series models were available, their GVW ratings, and the engine choices that were available in them.

A new model in the F Series line this year was the F-600 LPO. "LPO" stands for "Low Profile Option."

The F-600 LPO's primary feature was its low loading height of 32 inches, which was 6 inches lower than the loading height of a regular F-600 truck. This lower profile meant the truck was easier to load, which was a strong selling point to buyers like rental agencies who needed vehicles that offered easier loading.

When it was introduced at the start of the 1990 model year the F-600 LPO was made available in two wheelbase lengths. The shorter of the two was set at 207 inches while the longer version had a wheelbase length of 237 inches. These trucks came

1990 F Series Model Lineup

Model	GVW Ratings	Engines
F Super-Duty	16,000 lbs (max)	7.5L (460 cubic inch) V-8, 7.3L Diesel (option)
F-600 LPO	19,000-21,000 lbs	6.1L (370 cubic inch) V-8, 7.0L (429 cubic inch) V-8 (option)
F-600	22,000-26,500 lbs	6.1L (370 cubic inch) V-8, 7.0L (429 cubic inch) V-8 (option), 6.6L Ford Diesel In-Line 6 (option)
F-700	30,000 lbs	7.0L (429 cubic inch) V-8, 6.6L Ford Diesel In-Line 6 (option)
F-700 4x4	24,000 lbs	7.0L (429 cubic inch) V-8
F-800	35,000 lbs	7.0L (429 cubic inch) V-8, 6.6L Ford Diesel In-Line 6 (option)
FT-800	52,000 lbs	7.0L (429 cubic inch) V-8
FT-900	52,000 lbs	Ford Diesel Engine

equipped with 6.1L or 7.0L gasoline V-8 engines and those engines could be mated to either an Eaton FS3005A 5-speed manual transmission or an Allison AT 545 automatic transmission. Tires on these trucks were a low profile radial in a 19.5-inch size.

Later on in the model year Ford added a new F-700 LPO truck to the mix at the same time they added Ford Diesel engine options for these trucks. In addition to those changes Ford announced they were adding another shorter wheelbase chassis for these trucks. This new chassis model would have a 189-inch wheelbase.

Once again in this model year Ford offered their customers two ways to order these trucks. A customer could order a truck through Ford's "Work Ready" Program or they could order a truck through a "Custom Built Order" to custom tailor a truck to their needs. To get more participation in their "Work Ready" Program this year Ford offered "Flex Options." These "Flex Options" included a change in exterior color paint, wheel changes from disc to spoke type and vice versa, wheelbase changes from shorter to longer and vice versa, radial tires substituted for tube type tires, tube type tires replaced with tubeless tires, and air conditioning that could be added or deleted.

Those were positive changes for the 1990 Ford truck line but a negative point would emerge for

This Ford 1991 Cargo box van is used by the Greater Franklin County Tactical Rescue Squad of Missouri to perform trench rescue situations. *Dennis J. Maag*

A 1993 Smeal Pumper Body has been added to this 1992 Ford F-700 truck that is used by the St. Francis Fire Department of St. Francis, Kansas, to fight fires in that area. *Dennis J. Maag*

the line as the 1990 model year was starting to near its end when Ford announced that they were going to discontinue their ever-popular line of C Series Tilt Cab trucks — trucks that had been a mainstay of the line ever since they were introduced with the 1957 models.

This Ford F Series truck features the restyled front end that Ford adopted for these trucks starting in 1995.

This news must have come as a shock to makers of fire fighting and refuse equipment who liked these trucks because they fit their needs to a tee. In its place Ford offered their Cargo Tilt Cab trucks but the Cargo would never reach the high levels of popularity or acceptance that the Ford C Series Tilt Cab had enjoyed over a long period. Many in the industry thought Ford was making a big mistake by dropping this popular model. Unfortunately this wouldn't be the last mistake that Ford would make during the 1990s.

Except for the loss of the C Tilt Cab trucks the 1991 Ford truck lineup was pretty much the same as what was offered in 1990. However, there was one major change that involved Ford's Cargo trucks. Prior to the 1991 model year these trucks were built for the North American and Latin American markets at Ford's Ipiranga Truck Plant in Sao Paulo, Brazil. With the demise of the C Tilt Cabs Ford now had some extra room at their Kentucky Truck Plant and production of the North American market Cargos was moved from Brazil to the Kentucky Truck Plant. Ford had some free time between the last 1990 C Series Tilt Cab model being built and the start of the 1991 model year and they used up that time preparing to ramp up production for the 1991 Cargo. Cargo production for the Latin American market was still handled at the Brazil plant.

For 1992 Ford expanded their lineup of Low Profile Option, or LPO models, to four. These models were the F-600 LPO, the F-600 LPOG, the F-700 LPO, and the F-700 LPOG. Ford also offered these trucks in seven different wheelbases ranging from 153 up to 255 inches in length. GVW ratings were also increased to 28,000 lbs thanks to the use of heavier-duty rated springs and axles.

The cab design on these LPO model trucks was similar in design to the cabs used on lighter-duty F Series trucks rather than the cabs used on the regular F-600 and F-700 range. Ford made this cab change to make the transition smoother for drivers that were accustomed to driving lower rated trucks.

Another change seen on Ford F-600 and F-700 LPO trucks was that Ford now offered them with a choice of hydraulic or air brake systems.

Looking at one of these trucks makes one wonder how Ford could produce such a low profile truck in this medium-duty range. They were able to do so by using flat, sturdy frames, low profile wheels and tires, a low profile fuel tank, parabolic taper type leaf springs, and auxiliary rear springs to support the load and add stability to the chassis.

The base engine for these LPO trucks was now a 7.0L (429 cubic inch) EFI gasoline V-8 that was rated at 236 horsepower. Optional engines for these trucks included Ford's excellent 6.6L in-line 6-cylinder diesel engines rated at 165, 170, and 185 horsepower. Standard transmissions for these trucks were 5-speed manuals with 4- or 5-speed automatics as options. If you ordered an F-700 LPO model you could also order it with a 6-, 9-, or 10-speed manual transmission.

These trucks came standard with a tilting fiberglass one-piece front end to make it easier for

An ex-Ryder System Ford F Series truck sits outside a construction equipment supply yard in Northern New Mexico.

Ford was still in the School Bus Chassis Business in the mid 1990s as this photograph shows.

A slick-looking Econoline cab and chassis provides for a good basic foundation for this special hot air balloon chase crew truck.

routine maintenance.

By the time the 1993 model year rolled around Ford was deeply involved in developing and designing brand new heavy-duty and light-duty truck models as well as a new Mustang automobile so there was very little money available to spend on making changes to their medium-duty truck models. Any changes done to these trucks were

This Ford F Series truck from the mid-1990s is fitted with a modern tow truck body. It spends a lot of its time picking up cars in the Albuquerque, New Mexico, area.

probably minor in nature.

Pre-production of Ford's new "Louisville Line" of trucks began at the Kentucky Truck Plant in the 1994 model year. These new trucks were built alongside the older design L Series medium and heavy-duty trucks that had been built at the plant since it was opened.

During the latter part of the model year Ford opened a new Ford Commercial Truck Vehicle Center in Dearborn, Michigan. The primary objective in opening this new complex was to design, engineer, and market Ford trucks of all shapes and sizes for the North American, Latin American, European, and Asian Pacific markets.

This new facility was responsible for vehicles like the F Series trucks, Cargo trucks, B Series School Bus Chassis, Econoline vehicles, Ford transit vans, buses, and trucks for the European market, the P Series Chassis, Ford L Series, "Louisville Line," and AeroMax trucks.

For Ford's F Series line their new 1995 models featured the same cabs with different front-end treatments. Gone was its wide rectangular two-piece grille, which was now replaced with a higher, more square-looking grille that was placed in a modified housing. The front fender design was also changed taking on a wider, more organic shape. These fenders also had a swept back look with wraparound turning lamps that made them look wider still.

Ford's F and B Series trucks were put on redesigned frames this year as well.

Ford's redesigned "Louisville Line" of trucks debuted in 1995 as 1996 models. The same time these trucks were hitting the streets a new redesigned F Series of pickup trucks was released as 1997 models. Both of these new truck lines were sold alongside the older looking trucks for a period of time so that truck buyers had the choice between the old and the new. Both redesigned trucks were warmly received, which bode well for the future of Ford trucks. Then out of the blue

Ford announced they were selling off their Class 7 and Class 8 truck business to Freightliner, a division of DaimlerChrysler Corporation.

This news hit the Ford truck world like an atomic bomb. Nobody could understand how Ford, after spending millions of dollars and thousands of man hours designing and engineering these new trucks, could turn their backs on this end of the truck market. Ford claimed that the reason why they were taking this course of action was so that they could concentrate their efforts on producing more profitable models like sports utility vehicles. To do that they needed more assembly line space — assembly lines like those found at their Kentucky Truck Plant.

This major sale of assets wouldn't happen overnight and it would take almost two full years to complete but once it was done these new Ford trucks became Sterling.

The redesigned F Series trucks that were released for the 1995 model year stayed in production until they were replaced by Ford's new Super-Duty F Series models in 1998. These new trucks featured redesigned cabs and front ends that didn't look like the earlier models. By then the L Series of trucks were gone along with the B Series School Bus Chassis, and the Cargo as well.

These days you can get yourself a medium-duty Ford truck in the F Series Super-Duty line with models like the F-450, F-550, F-650, and the F-750. And some Econoline Chassis models also fit into this category. Times have surely changed from years ago when Ford was the undisputed leader in the Medium-Duty range thanks in large part to the wide range of models they offered in all their truck lines. These days the Medium-Duty truck market has a lot of trucks from more manufacturers vying for customers and it's hard to say who leads this market segment today.

By outfitting this U-Haul Ford F Series truck with an LPO option the person who rents this truck will have an easier time loading it.

This diesel engine powered Ford F Series truck makes a lot of stops everyday delivering beer to restaurants and bars.

This photograph shows a new late model Ford F-650 Super-Duty truck that has been fitted with a water tanker body.

This Ford F-650 Super Cab with a long wheelbase chassis has been fitted with a long aftermarket stake body.

The hamlet of Los Ranchos, New Mexico, just took delivery of this new Ford F-450 Crew Cab truck equipped with a special body full of brush fire fighting equipment.

The looks of the newest Ford F Series Super-Duty trucks take a while to get used to. This is an F-650 model with a tow truck body mounted on its chassis.

Kentucky Truck Plant

Ford's Kentucky Truck Plant opened its doors back in the fall of 1969 and the first vehicle out of those doors was Ford's brand new Louisville, or "L" Series Ford truck. The L Series was a truck that would become a sales leader and innovator in the Medium-Duty and Heavy-Duty truck world.

Located on 415 acres of land on the outskirts of Louisville, Kentucky, Ford would call this sprawling complex their Kentucky Truck Plant. When it opened this Kentucky Truck Plant was the world's largest and most modern commercial truck production facility. Its 68 acres under one roof provides more than 3 million square feet of manufacturing space devoted to the manufacture and assembly of trucks. When opened this facility consisted of a large data processing center, a hospital, a chassis dynamometer, a test track, a deep dip electrocoat primer paint bath, paint booths, and of course, three separate assembly lines for truck production. Since its opening more than 35 years ago Ford has spent millions of dollars improving and expanding this complex so that they could build better trucks and more of them.

Besides building Ford's L Series trucks at this facility other trucks like Ford's C Series Tilt Cabs, F-Series, W Series, CL Series, B Series School Bus Chassis, AeroMax, and Cargo Series trucks have been built here.

Over the years this plant has been responsible for producing millions of Ford trucks for Ford truck buyers and Ford truck enthusiasts to admire for years to come.

Robot welding rigs assemble a new Ford truck cab at Ford's Kentucky Truck Plant in Louisville, Kentucky. *Ford Motor Company Photograph*

As assembly line worker installs a dashboard assembly into a new Ford cab at the Kentucky Truck Plant. *Ford Motor Company Photograph*

Brand new Ford trucks, both heavy and medium-duty units, come down the assembly line at Ford's Kentucky Truck Plant. *Ford Motor Company Photograph*

Assembly line workers work on last minute details on a cab before it moves on to the primer dip bath at the Kentucky Truck Plant. *Ford Motor Company Photograph*

This photograph shows the special trim used on the 1948-1950 Canadian Mercury trucks. *Larry Heister*

If you are looking for a Ford truck that doesn't look like a Ford, then you might want to try to find a 1952 Mercury truck like the one shown in this magazine ad. *Michael MacSems Collection*

Catalog cover used on the 1960 Mercury Medium-Duty truck catalog. Check out that unique trim.

The Mercury Connection

Elsewhere in this book we talked about Ford of Canada offering a Mercury truck for their Mercury dealers to sell. These trucks used the same bodies, drivetrains, frames, and such as their Ford counterparts that were sold at Ford dealerships throughout the United States, Latin America, Canada, and other markets. What made the Mercury trucks look different were their unique trim pieces that set them apart from other Ford vehicles.

These trucks were first offered in 1946 and continued in production through the 1968 model year when Ford of Canada decided to end their production.

If you want a Ford truck that looks a little different you may want to consider finding yourself a Mercury. However, be forewarned that these trucks were built in far lesser numbers than regular Ford trucks so they are a lot harder to come by. Still if you want something different this is a good way to go. On that same note some Ford trucks, especially the F Series versions for the Latin American market, were also produced with different trim than Ford F Series trucks we have seen here in the United States. So once again, if you want something that looks different and you are in South America, you may want to look for a Latin American edition of an F Series truck.

Ford Truck Historical Timeline

1917: Ford Model T One-Ton Truck Chassis Introduced. Officially starting Ford in the truck business.

1922: Electric Start Option Introduced For Ford Trucks. With this option you didn't need to hand crank your Model TT truck anymore.

1924: Ford Begins Producing Model TT Trucks with Open Cabs and Express Bodies.

1925: Ford Introduces the Model T Runabout with Pickup Body Option. This was Ford's first pickup truck. Ford also started offering a Closed Cab version of their Model TT trucks this year.

1928: Model AA 1 1/2-Ton Truck Replaces Model T One-Ton Truck, or Model TT.

1932: Model BB Ford Trucks Replace Model AA Ford Trucks. Ford also introduces their L-Head V-8 engine option for cars and trucks.

1933: For The First Time Ford Car and Truck Styling Is Separated. Some cars would be restyled every year while trucks would maintain the same style for years in some cases.

1934: The Last Year For Open Cab Ford Truck Models and For 4-Cylinder Engines For Awhile.

1935: Marmon-Herrington Starts Modifying Ford 2-Wheel-Drive Trucks Into All-Wheel-Drive Units.

1938: Ford Adds Cab-Over-Engine Models To Go Along With Their Regular Models.

1940: Hotchkiss Type Rear End Replaces Torque Tube Type Rear Axles On Ford Heavy Trucks.

1941: Ford Introduces A New 6-Cylinder Engine Option For Their Cars And Trucks. Some Ford pickups available with 4-cylinder engines as well.

1942: Civilian Car And Truck Production Ceases In February of 1942 So Ford Can Concentrate All Their Efforts On The War.

1943-1944: Ford Introduces Their GTP Military Vehicles Alongside Their Other War Vehicles.

1945: Limited Civilian Car And Truck Production Begins Again.

1946: Ford Offers 2-Ton Rated Trucks Alongside Their 1 1/2-Ton Regular Models.

1948: Ford F-Series "Bonus Built" Trucks Introduced.

1949: Ford Introduces Their New Parcel Delivery Chassis.

1953: Ford Introduces Their New "Economy Series" Of Trucks. Cab-Over-Engine trucks become "Cab Forward Trucks" and they get their own series when the C Series is born.

1956: Ford Restyles Their Economy Trucks and The Result Becomes A Classic. Ford pushes safety aspect of their vehicles and switches from 6-volt electrical systems to 12 volt.

1957: Totally Redesigned Ford F Series Trucks Introduced. The C Series Tilt Cabs Also Introduced. Ford also releases a car/truck hybrid they call the Ranchero.

1961: Ford Introduces A Restyled F Series Line Of Trucks Along With a New "H Series" and A New Econoline Series.

1963: Ford Introduces A New "N" Series of Trucks And Also Releases Diesel Powered City Delivery Truck Engine Option.

1966: Ford Introduces A New Utility Vehicle They Call The Bronco.

1967: New "W" Series Of Trucks Replace the "H" Series And Ford Restyles Their F Series.

1968: New Ford Truck Operations Unit Created.

1969: Ford Opens A Brand New Truck Plant That They Call Their Kentucky Truck Plant.

1970: Ford Introduces Their New Louisville Series Of Medium And Heavy-Duty Trucks, Which Replace Ford's "N" Series.

1973: Redesigned F Series Truck Debuts And The Second Series Of Ford's "W" Series Debuts.

1978: Ford Replaces Their "W" Series Of Trucks With Their New "CL" Series. Bronco also gets bigger and more popular this year.

1980: New Aerodynamically Restyled Ford F Series Trucks Released, Ford Also Introduces A Factory LPG Conversion For Their Gasoline Fueled Engines.

1986: Ford Introduces Their New Cargo Tilt Cab Models To The USA Market.

1990: C Series Tilt Cab Trucks Discontinued After 33-Year Run. Ford introduces their new Explorer Sport Utility Vehicle.

1991: Cargo Truck Production Moves To The Kentucky Truck Plant For North American Markets.

1994: Commercial Truck Vehicle Center Formed In Dearborn, Michigan, To Design And Market Ford Trucks Worldwide. Two Millionth Truck Built at the Kentucky Truck Plant.

1995: A Restyled F Series Of Trucks Emerge And Ford Builds Their Restyled "Louisville Line" And AeroMax Trucks.

1996: Ford Announces Their Intention To Sell Their Class 7 And Class 8 Truck Assets And Business to Freightliner.

1998: Ford Class 7 and Class 8 Trucks Now Become Sterlings After Deal With Freightliner Finalized.

1998: Ford Announces Their New F Series Super-Duty Lineup. Heaviest-Duty Ford Trucks Are Now the F-650 and F-750 With The Demise Of Ford's "L" Series Line.

Epilogue

Over the course of the last 87 years Ford has built millions of Medium-Duty trucks and if you are interested in finding one to collect you should not have any problem finding one you like.

If you are interested in simplicity you can't find a simpler truck than the Model TT truck. You can buy them already restored or buy them as project vehicles. Parts can still be found at swap meets and from dealers across the country.

If your tastes run to a more stylish truck with more comfort and convenience items then you'll probably want to look for a Model AA truck. These trucks were offered in both Open Cab and Closed Cab forms with quite a variety of factory and aftermarket bodies. These trucks are more popular with collectors. Parts, like those for the Model TT, are easy to find at swap meets and from parts dealers. Or you can save yourself the trouble and buy one already restored.

For those of you who need a more powerful truck with a V-8 engine than a Ford truck from 1932 this is the way to go. Not only did they have more power but also they offered the buyer more equipment and models to choose from. As an added bonus in the late 1930s Ford started offering these trucks in Regular Cab or Cab-Over-Engine models. More Regular Cabs were built and they are easier to find but if you want one that looks different hold out for a COE model. And if you want one that is really rare look for a Marmon-Herrington All-Wheel-Drive Ford.

Ford built a lot of good-looking trucks in the 1940s offering the truck collector lots of trucks from which to choose. These include trucks from just before and after the war, and the popular "Bonus Built" F Series trucks of the late 1940s. Parts for these trucks are relatively easy to find if you want to restore one yourself or you can buy one already finished. Don't forget the Canadian Mercury trucks from this era if you want a really rare truck.

Like the 1940s Ford offered a lot of choices of new trucks during the 1950s. You can choose from the "Bonus Built" F Series trucks of the early 1950s, a "Classic" big fendered Ford from the 1953 to 1956 period, a Tilt Cab C Series, or a redesigned F Series truck with slab sided styling from the late 1950s. Or

you can go for one of those Mercury trucks from Canada. Once again, parts are easy to find for restorers or you can find lots of completed trucks on the market today.

When it comes to choices in big Ford trucks you can't beat the 1960s. At the start of the decade you have a restyled F Series line that you can choose from. Or you can pick one of the "N" Series Fords that came out in 1963 with either a gasoline or a diesel engine for power. If you like Tilt Cab trucks the C Series Ford still had a lot to offer and if you want a truck that looks really "macho" you can always go with an F Series truck from the latter part of the decade. You probably won't have any trouble finding most parts for these trucks if you want to fix one up. Or you can just buy a truck that has been restored or one that is still in good operating condition.

In the 1970s besides the regular F and C Series trucks you have the "Louisville Line" or "L" Series that you can choose from. There are literally thousands of these trucks still on the road so you should have no problem finding one to buy and fix up. Some Ford truck dealers still stock parts for these trucks.

If you like aerodynamic looking trucks then the 1980s is the era you'll want to look at. You can find sleek looking Ford F and L Series trucks or if you want a truck with European styling you can choose a Cargo Tilt Cab model. You can still find these trucks working every day and parts are pretty easy to find at your Ford dealers.

What we said for Ford's 1980 offerings can also be said for their 1990 era trucks. Ford offered all sorts of redesigned trucks from this era so finding one that suits your tastes or needs is pretty easy to do. Though some of you might think these trucks are too new to collect today they will be collectible in years to come.

As you can see from what you read in this book no matter what sort of Medium-Duty truck you wanted Ford always had something to offer no matter what the year or the decade. If you already have a Ford truck cherish it, or if you don't, go out and buy one, or two.

Happy Hunting And Keep On Ford Trucking!